Anarchism

Focus on Contemporary Issues (FOCI) addresses the pressing problems, ideas and debates of the new millennium. Subjects are drawn from the arts, sciences and humanities, and are linked by the impact they have had or are having on contemporary culture. FOCI books are intended for an intelligent, alert audience with a general understanding of, and curiosity about, the intellectual debates shaping culture today. Instead of easing readers into a comfortable awareness of particular fields, these books are combative. They offer points of view, take sides and are written with passion.

SERIES EDITORS
Barrie Bullen and Peter Hamilton

In the same series

Cool Rules
Dick Pountain and David Robins

Chromophobia
David Batchelor

Global Dimensions
John Rennie Short

Celebrity
Chris Rojek

Activism!
Tim Jordan

Animal
Erica Fudge

Dreamtelling
Pierre Sorlin

Anarchism

SEÁN M. SHEEHAN

REAKTION BOOKS

Published by Reaktion Books Ltd
79 Farringdon Road
London EC1M 3JU, UK

www.reaktionbooks.co.uk

First published 2003

Printed and bound in Great Britain by
Biddles Ltd, Guildford and King's Lynn

British Library Cataloguing in Publishing Data
Sheehan, Seán, M. 1951–
    Anarchism. – (FOCI)
    1. Anarchism 2. Anarchism – History
    I. Title
    335.8'3

ISBN 1 86189 169 5

Contents

CHAPTER ONE

Global Anarchism

The New Anarchism

Seattle, November 1999. The Carnival Against Capital. The World Trade Organization (WTO) arrived in Seattle on the evening of 29 November, and thousands of protestors waited to meet the delegates arriving at the Exhibition Center in their limousines and coaches. The first march through Seattle started at 6 am the next morning, and by the afternoon street blockades were still holding their own, aided and abetted by street theatre and pavement parties. Wednesday morning saw more protestors gathering at 7 am, though the response was also more determined, and armoured personnel carriers appeared on the streets. Friday witnessed large groups of non-violent protestors mounting a sit-down outside the city gaol, where arrested demonstrators were being detained. Each evening, meetings took place, with representatives of different affinity groups sitting together in large circles to discuss tactics. The warehouse building where these meetings were held had for days leading up to 29 November been the venue for non-violence training sessions and gaol solidarity workshops; and once the action got under way, *ad hoc* first aid sessions were the order of the day. Throughout the five days of protest, key anarchist principles were seen to work so successfully that other non-anarchist militants adopted them. No centralized authority or hierarchical bureaucracy emerged, and yet a remarkable degree of coordination developed as affinity groups organized a wide range of activities, including marches, human blockade chains, banner displays, street props and pavement theatre. Participants of all persuasions were welcomed at the anarchist Convergence Center, which served as a clearing house for a variety of organizational needs, from help with accommodation to medical care and plans for new forms of agitation. Communication was effected through a combination of mobile phones, large notices at the Convergence Center, and even messages emblazoned on T-shirts.

Black flags were to be seen flying though the acrid smoke, but when a McDonald's outlet was stormed it was rounds of Roquefort cheese that hit the plate glass windows. Not for the first time at an anti-capitalist protest, many traditional idioms of revolution – guns, bombs and armies – were playfully deconstructed in a potent commitment to peaceful and photogenic protest. Activists appeared in mock 'uniforms' of anonymous white overalls and chemical suits. In Prague, almost a year after Seattle, protesting against the International Monetary Fund (IMF), mini armies of protestors came dressed as fairies and armed with feather dusters to tickle the ranks of heavily clothed, armed police. At such protests, lines of transport tend to be blocked not so much by burning barricades and street battles but by giant contraptions like the Liberation Puppet, capable of snarling up a major highway. Protest in Quebec City in 2001 included a mock medieval catapult that fired an array of soft toys over the heads of the lines of police protecting the FTAA (Free Trade Area of the Americas) delegates. At the 2000 Republican National Convention in Philadelphia, protestors attired themselves as gross parodies of billionaires and dictators, and the Radical Cheerleaders called for a radical feminism dressed in saucy skirts and pompons. Some of these antics seem harmless enough, but the anti-capitalist movement, far from being an innocuous throwback to the protests of the 1960s, heralds a new movement for radical change in the twenty-first century, one that engages with an anarchism re-emerging from a period of dormancy.

Five days of largely peaceful insurgency by a 75,000-strong group of protestors had brought a scheduled conference of the WTO close to collapse. Reclaim the Streets-style happenings asserted car-less people's rights to control public spaces, while Black Bloc anarchists, and the easily recognized Ya Basta ('Enough Already') in their tute bianche ('white over-alls'), shared pavement space with French and Korean farmers, youth groups, environmentalists, pacifists, steelworkers, protestors against biotech foods and a host of other groups. They broadly shared a common objective, to protest vigorously at global injustices for which they held the WTO responsible, and protestors succeeded in bringing their concerns into the public domain in a way never seen before. The media could not help but record non-violent demonstrators being attacked by snatch squads and Darth Vader-like myrmidons firing rubber bullets and wielding batons, tear-gas, pepper sprays and concussion grenades. That the size and organization of the protests spooked the police into frenzied and blatantly illegal behaviour was confirmed by the fact that of the 631 arrests, only 14 ever went to trial. While Seattle erupted, with an early success that saw the WTO's opening being cancelled, public protests were taking place across France, in Amsterdam, Berlin, Buenos Aires, Colombo, Geneva, in India, Manila and Milan.

The international media loved the Seattle event because the highly visual spectacle also provided more traditional images of mayhem, as when Starbucks, Planet Hollywood and Nike stores were attacked. Here was an opportunity for the media to resurrect the spectre of anarchism and demonize anarchist protestors as demented and dangerous, beyond the pale, donning face-masks to run amok, hurl paving stones and indulge in an orgy of looting. What was more difficult to explain was the minor role of these relatively small groups of protestors when put alongside the other anarchist groups, pacifists, farmers, trade unionists and environmentalists who came together as natural allies in five days of sustained and highly organized non-violent protest. What baffled the media was the fact that there was no single group or leader behind an orchestrated and tightly arranged campaign that saw small groups split off to blockade streets and hotels and prevent delegates reaching their meetings. Even the attacks on property that did occur involved stores that had been deliberately targeted because of the way their symbolic and material role is seen to reflect the nature of a free-market fundamentalism colonizing the world.[1] Roquefort cheese, for example, was chosen because it was one of the European products on which the US imposed a retaliatory 100 per cent surcharge when Europe refused to import hormone-treated beef from the US.

Seattle came as a shock to mainstream politicos and armchair apparatchiks, as well as to the media. Where did the thousands of protestors come from? What party or group did they subscribe to? The roots of the anti-capitalist movement, which go back 30 years to anti-Vietnam War protests and, later, anti-nuclear power rallies, were as largely unknown as were the anti-hierarchical, anarchist-inspired structures – affinity groups, spokescouncils, consensus decision-making – that informed the organizational success of the Seattle event; and, being unknown, the structures were not understood as the embodiment of libertarian organization. Originating with anarchists in the Spanish Civil War of the 1930s, affinity groups are the self-empowered units that operate at an atomic level across the gamut of activities – from passive chains of demonstrators to theatre groups and activists prepared to face arrest – and a spokescouncil is formed from affinity group representatives. Both spokesperson and a spoke in the organizational wheel, the representatives speak for their groups and coordinate the flexible clusters of affinity groups before and during an event. Decision-making at every level is participatory and democratic, always allowing for dissent and with procedures that have been developed to accommodate minority opinions and facilitate conflict resolution.

And what was the Seattle rainbow of black, red and green protesting at?[2] The Cold War was over, nuclear annihilation a seemingly past issue, and yet here was a controlled explosion of dissent. The protests did not emanate from parties of the political left, or at least not in the traditional sense, for such parties were singularly absent from Seattle. The institutionalized left had not planned this event, but the very conscious solidarity that ran through the spectrum of protestors was left-wing and libertarian in both spirit and organization. The protests at Seattle opposed organizations like the WTO, the World Bank and the IMF because they are seen as the very real but shadowy heart of global capitalism, a super-executive that transcends the nation-state. The institutions directing and imposing the economic policies for a new world order are unelected, unaccountable and international, and anarchism – a political and social radicalism that opposes capitalism with a libertarian communism – has re-emerged in recent years as a response to global neoliberalism. The free-market economic framework that underpins neoliberalism is rationalized by its ideologues as a democratic capitalism that provides everyone with an equal opportunity to succeed and prosper. Anarchists are not alone in asserting, to the contrary, that in reality the discourse of neoliberalism is a theoretical gloss that disguises economic control by a privileged elite and, in its global ambitions, speaks for a new form of colonialism. This economic neo-colonialism allows an international class of capitalists and certain nations, principally the US, to turn entire communities of people into economic satellites, with organizations like the WTO to police and monitor these satellite states. During the Cold War, any such pointed criticism of capitalism conveniently allowed defenders of the free market to gesture to inequities in the Soviet system and saddle critics with the opprobrium of being labelled a Communist. The rules of engagement have now shifted because the anti-capitalist movement is not about capturing political power in the traditional sense and it is not Communist in the traditional sense either. Principled opposition to capitalism is usually associated with left-wing ideologies and the national political parties that uphold them, but there were no such parties behind the protests at Seattle. What activists seek is not the capture of seats in a parliament but the dismantling of the ideas and practices of a free market ideology that aggressively insists on shaping human history in its own selfish image. The movement places its faith in grass roots organization and – a consequence of the globalization that has brought it into existence – protests on the international stage. Part of the history of the movement that took Seattle by storm began in the global South, with the 1996 International Encounter for Humanity and Against Neoliberalism held in Zapatista-held Chiapas in Mexico, and a declaration of intent to form a new network of dissent.

> A network of voices that not only speaks but also struggles and resists for humanity and against neoliberalism.
> A network that covers the five continents and helps to resist the death that Power promises us.
> A network without a central head or decision maker: it has no central command or hierarchies. We are the network, all of us who resist.[3]

The model for the kind of political and social autonomy that the anti-capitalist movement aspires to is an anarchist one, and the soul of the anti-capitalist movement is anarchist; its non-authoritarian make-up, its disavowal of traditional parties of the left, and its commitment to direct action are firmly in the spirit of libertarian socialism. The movement seeks to short-circuit the trans-global corporations that are themselves beginning to take on aspects of the state and, in the process, 'First worlders may find particular inspiration in the possibility of alliances with third and fourth world activists.'[4]

The fundamental critique of free market economics that the anti-capitalist movement espouses has a lot in common with a Marxist analysis of the existing social and economic order, and the relationship between

Marxism and anarchism is the subject of chapter Three. There are close overlaps between anarchism and Marxism, given that the genealogy of libertarian communism includes an analysis of capitalism, focusing on its exploitative logic and its corrosive effect on human relations in a way that goes back to Marx's early writings. Marx's account of alienation, of people's unhappy and unfulfilled existence under capitalism, is also common to both communism and anarchism. The evolutionary progress of Marxism and anarchism follows the same radical path of questioning the social and political effects of the capitalist economic system. Where they differ is over the best way of challenging and changing the existing order, and this is reflected in the way that the anti-capitalist movement, while it takes on board aspects of Marx's analysis of the free market, has very firmly divorced itself from the Marxism of Lenin and state socialism.

The Anarchist Turn

All this is a long way from the traditional image of anarchism as a synonym for nihilism and wilful, Dostoyevskian destruction. Such a stereotype was nurtured by anarchist-inspired acts of assassination around the late nineteenth century, and with victims like Tsar Alexander II, French President Carnot and US President McKinley it is not surprising that the image of the anarchist as a deranged, bewhiskered homicide took hold. The Press was happy to conjoin anarchism, socialism and terrorist violence, and a number of popular films and novels played with stereotypes of anarchism as an irrational, destructive impulse. Joseph Conrad's novel *The Secret Agent* (1907) involved a fictional community of London anarchists that include the character Karl Yundt with a 'swaggering tilt to a black felt sombrero shading the hollows and ridges of his wasted face'. But Yundt is eclipsed by the unhinged Professor who carries a bomb in his pocket and whose motto is 'No God! No Master!' The Professor has a bomb that will explode just twenty seconds after its activation, but, unsatisfied with the mechanism, he labours long hours in his laboratory to make the 'perfect detonator'. Echoing Archimedes, he boasts: 'Madness and despair! Give me that for a lever, and I'll move the world.' The novel ends with the Professor skulking through the streets of London,

> averting his eyes from the odious multitude of mankind. He had no future. He disdained it. He was a force. His thoughts caressed the images of ruin and destruction. He walked frail, insignificant, shabby, miserable – and terrible in the simplicity of his idea calling madness and despair to the regeneration of the world. Nobody looked at him. He passed on unsuspected and deadly, like a pest in the street full of men.[5]

Early films of the twentieth century also played with the image of the sinister anarchist as an icon of irrationality, and the bohemian trimmings that usually defined such a figure ensured he could not be imagined as having anything in common with the kind of citizens watching such films. As late as 1960, Robert Baker's *The Siege of Sidney Street* was able to recycle some familiar stereotypes in a film depicting an event of 1911 that saw a shoot-out in the heart of London's East End between police and bank robbers who were characterized – erroneously in fact – as anarchists. In the film the robbers are politically motivated, and although they never identify themselves as anarchists, they hang out in a club that a local barman, gossiping with an undercover policeman, describes as the haunt of 'anarchists, atheists and vegetarians'. A key member of the gang, Peter the Painter, is played by Peter Wyngarde as a sincere but ruthless ideologue, while another gang member, the odious, knife-wielding Yoska, takes a grim delight in his own gratuitous violence and sexual aggressiveness. The cockney neighbourhood in which they live comprises apolitical rubbernecks who gather to watch the final shoot-out as state power, under the direction of toffs in top hats, including a cigar-smoking Home Secretary (Winston Churchill was the minister at the time and he did indeed make an appearance in Sidney Street), combats what is portrayed as an utterly un-English eruption of political violence. In the mid-1970s, Claude Chabrol's thriller *Nada* had a more contemporary setting – the fictional, bungled kidnapping of the US ambassador to France – but made no attempt to nuance the image of the anarchist as a fanatical iconoclast dressed in black. In the film, Buenaventure Diaz, the Spanish leader of the kidnap gang, is a smartened-up version of the wild and bearded bohemian Peter the Painter in *The Siege of Sidney Street*. Diaz, who is fashionably attired in a long black leather coat, cool sombrero and a neatly trimmed beard, even shouts 'Long live Death!'[6] Chabrol's film has a degree of complexity – or cynicism at least – that harks back to the moral equivalence of terrorism and the state's willingness to murder that is found in Conrad's novel, but anarchism as a distinctive creed is given little attention. Diaz, alive but alone after his comrades have been killed after a police raid on the farmhouse where the ambassador was being held, speaks to the camera and acknowledges that terrorist violence only reinforces the power of the state – 'the state hates terrorism, but prefers it to revolution' – but says nothing that even hints at the creative richness of the anarchist project.

What are the essential convictions of anarchist thought? Anarchism is revolutionary in that it desires a new social order based on libertarian socialist ideas. There is a principled opposition to most forms of imposed, centralized or hierarchical authority. Institutions and organizations and structures of thought and art in culture that embody such forms of authority are criticized and rejected because they are seen to inhibit, control or repress the creative and productive abilities of people. Anarchism, far from evoking an imaginary time before the Fall, is very much about people taking responsibility for their workaday lives and sets itself the challenge of developing forms of participatory, democratic government for modern, complex societies. The difficulties facing attempts to create a libertarian and decentralized social order are not minimized ('And if everyone were to want to eat partridge and drink wine from the Chianti district . . . who will empty the privies?' asks the anarchist Errico Malatesta[7]), and anarchism is acutely aware of the problems in developing co-ordinated, decision-making structures without at the same time creating a bureaucracy that contains the seeds of the very authoritarianism it seeks to replace. Pro-localization, the positive face of what is sometimes called the anti-globalization movement, means seeking to create decentralized communities where power is not allowed to concentrate in the hands of an elite or a bureaucracy.

Principles may remain constant, but history changes the times, and anarchism has turned to meet the challenge. Revolutionary politics in the nineteenth and twentieth centuries looked to the violent overthrow of existing governments as the means to change the nature of society. Nowadays, ironically, the source of such a revolutionary politics is the US, as it uses its unchallenged status as the world's only superpower to export neoliberalism around the world by violently threatening, and if necessary deposing, states that refuse to kowtow to its economic priorities. An inversion of sorts is taking place as neoliberalism, made manifest by US foreign policy, increasingly shows its willingness to use massive physical violence to intimidate states reluctant to accept US hegemony, while the new anarchism of the anti-capitalist movement is developing an agenda of *détournement* that overturns conventional notions of radical insurrection. By their methods of protest and their symbolic gestures, the anti-capitalist movement represents an anarchist-inspired opposition to neoliberalism. And sometimes the symbolism combines with pragmatism. Ya Basta, which began in Italy in 1996 as an act of leaderless solidarity in response to the Zapatista uprising in Mexico, chose white overalls to represent the state of powerless invisibility that people are reduced to under neo-liberal policies, but their Michelin Man attire of pads, helmets and shields is also there to protect them from police violence.

Many anarchists, though not all, are coming to accept that the anti-capitalist movement will be necessarily non-violent in order to viably challenge and confront the organized violence of the post-Cold War, US-led alliance of nation states that promote and sustain international capital and market Stalinism. Organized violence leading to war has always characterized nation state behaviour – and the ruling classes of the last 100 years have been the most violent and destructive in history – with Communist and capitalist states adopting the same machinery of war and similar methods of both policing and practising state-sanctioned violence. The new era of global capitalism sees the same use of violence on an international stage, using the UN, NATO or the adroitly flexible 'war on terrorism', and opposition to this in the form of violent protest is doomed both in principle and practice. Anarchism opposes the central-ized, hierarchical mind-set that informs and structures the power of the state, and this, necessarily, involves a rejection of the organized violence that states embody. The use of paint-bombs not semtex, water pistols not guns, and the employment of mock armies of fairies or white-overalled protestors, ludicrously emboldened by foam padding or elongated rubber limbs, is not the expression of a soft, hippy gradualism but a dramatically visual form, appropriate to public dissent, of a non-hierarchical opposi-tional movement up in arms. The anarchist principles that inspire the carnivalesque disruption of order at summit meetings and elsewhere are the same principles that inform the non-hierarchical forms of organiza-tion of the anti-capitalist movement as a whole and its proposals for economic and political change. At the same time, though, this does not mean that anarchism is blind to the fact that the capitalist order will use violence to defend its interests. Anarchists stress the difference between the monstrous violence of governments and the confrontational approach and property destruction adopted by some groups of anti-capitalist protestors. Chapter Four looks at the seemingly unresolvable relationship between anarchism and violence.

The most common negative response to anarchism is that its utopian idealism places it on the far side of any existing or even imaginable state of affairs. If we awoke one apocalyptic morning to discover that government has been abolished, then questions such as *Who will empty the dustbins?* and *Who will catch murderers?* would seem to render talk of anarchism absurd; quixotic at best and menacing nonsense at worst. Evoking anarchy in such terms confuses anarchism as a synonym for dangerous chaos with anarchism as a programme for radical changes in the way we live. There is an unavoidable elasticity to the use of the term anarchy that is the source of confusion on the subject and, with this in mind, the following chapter sets out the key strands of anarchism as a serious political and social philosophy. At the heart of anarchist thought is the conviction that people should determine their own future, based on their freedom, dignity and creativeness, and live and work within an economic system that allows them to control their destiny as far as possible. Neoliberalism is seen as a mockery of just such beliefs by its reduction of too many areas of life to a universal set of market transactions, so that almost everything has a price and very little has a value. The opposition that anarchism brings to this economics and the ethics it creates has its philosophical roots in the ground that Marx prepared when he saw that human nature is not static. Marx and anarchists share the Promethean conviction that humanity possesses an unlimited ability to self-create and bring into existence a new reality. For just as capitalism overthrew feudalism and made a new world, and as it now seeks to extend this world of the market into the heart and soul of third and fourth world communities, there is in principle nothing to prevent the possibility of radical change overthrowing this world, creating a new economics and different values. Anarchism shares with Marx this dynamic, revolutionary belief in the power that comes from the contingent nature of history. The recognition that reality is what we make it and that new realities are always being forged is the foundation of a powerful social ontology, and this is the concern of chapter Three.

The libertarian ideal, like all ideals, is utopian, but it doesn't follow that the idea of anarchism as a workable basis for civilized and organized activity is only of theoretical interest. The very real existence of the internet, with its borderless and ownerless architecture, serves as a paradigm of anarchism in this respect. When it started in the early 1990s, the internet was premised on the unlicensed sharing of the core resources that made the system technologically feasible. Significant innovations affecting the internet – the World Wide Web for browsing, email, online chatting – have come from individuals working independently of the system as a whole and not seeking to control it. No one owns the internet, and the success of an ownerless and unpoliceable enterprise can still take people by surprise, rather in the way that Buddhism surprises by being a religion without a god.

It is too easy, though, to spout holistic baloney about the internet, for while it demonstrates the workability of some key anarchist principles, its history also embodies the familiar way in which the power of capital seeks to exploit and control new resources. It is already the case that a very small number of sites, like Microsoft and America Online (AOL), have a dominating influence over surfing time, hardly a coincidence given Microsoft's control of the consumer operating system and AOL's dominance of subscriber lists and its hefty input into web content. When it started to take off around 1994–5, the internet's message was an electronic version of Mao's joyful invitation to let a hundred flowers blossom, but its subsequent history shows signs of mirroring the descent of Mao's liberating gospel into centralized and authoritarian control.[8] The internet's astonishing growth and popularity depended on the ability of computer users to connect to local telephone lines. Telephone companies did not have a right to refuse or limit internet service providers (ISPs) gaining access to telephone wires. The internet thrived because of the open access to the humble telephone line. Now that this physical platform is about to be replaced by a faster broadband technology – cable, for instance – it is possible that control of content will be introduced at an early stage in a way that telephone companies were never allowed to do. Cable companies, unlike their predecessors the telephone companies, are able to control access to their system. The law is being used, and changed, in other ways to control the open-ended architecture of the internet. Napster, using the internet to share music with other users, met its fate in US law courts and lost out to a music industry that has five companies monopolizing over 80 per cent of music distribution in the world. The open nature of the internet is also being reined in by other means, as anyone who experienced the system a few years ago can testify. Five or more years ago, surfing the web was a journey into the unknown and there was no way of predicting where one link might lead to; nowadays, with weblogs and search engines listing sites on the basis of popularity, a collectivist consciousness is in danger of cyberrailing use of the web's anarchic architecture.

At the same time, though, the internet has become the locality for counter-resistance in the form of hacktivism – politically fuelled hacking by 'cyboteurs' – and, more profoundly, the internet has shown itself to be an ideal medium for anarchist-orientated groups and organizations intent on publicizing their ideas and movements. The most productive instance of this is the Indymedia phenomenon, a decentralized and open network of counter-information based around collectives of activists, artists and DIY media workers. Emerging from the anti-capitalist movement, the first Independent Media Center was formed in 1999 after Seattle and received some 1.5 million hits in its first week.[9] It is now truly intra-continental, with nearly 100 sites around the world, supporting each other and all inviting activists opposed to capitalism to directly upload video-, audio- and textfiles. In the same endeavour of merging form with content, anti-state insurgents have 'wired' their own organizations and not only reached out to a wider audience than was ever previously possible but, in turn, have found their own activities and programmes being affected in the process. This is true of the anti-capitalist movement as a whole, and

in the particular case of the Zapatista uprising in Mexico proved so astonishingly successful that the US Army commissioned a study, published in
1998, into the nature of the new beast they could see themselves having
to face in the future.[10] One of the study's conclusions was that the high
degree of internetting between social activists within and outside of
Mexico allowed a 'swarming' of support, both physical and electronic, to
take place after the Zapatista's declaration of revolt in 1994. This swarming was not premeditated, unlike the act of rebellion itself, and it changed
the nature of the uprising from a conventional insurgency into something
the study labelled 'a social netwar'. On-line activists made a vital, and
possibly crucial, difference to the nature and course of the Zapatista
uprising, with Mexico's foreign minister observing in 1995 (notwithstanding possible relief on his part) that 'Chiapas . . . is a place where there has
not been a shot fired in the last fifteen months . . . The shots lasted ten
days, and ever since the war has been a war of ink, of written word, a war
on the Internet.'[11] Chapter Four examines this in the context of the
history of anarchist-inspired revolts.

It is not surprising that the internet should itself be the site of resistance, for the history of anarchism is a tale of struggle between libertarian
impulses and subsequent attempts to rein them in alongside traditional
structures of authority from where they can be contained and subdued.
While the story of anarchism as a self-conscious philosophy has its beginnings in the nineteenth century, its antecedents in acts and ideas of
human autonomy go back to myths like the decision made by Eve and
Adam to disobey their master in Eden. The very real and very rich tapes-
try of libertarian thought that has informed our intellectual history is an
impressive and exuberant one, going back to Taoism and Buddhism. Its
internationalist heritage has been joyfully charted by Peter Marshall in
Demanding the Impossible (1993), and there is an immense library of literature that bears testimony to the appeal of anarchist ideas.[12]

Anarchist ideas can clearly be identified in the politics of the English

Civil Wars of the 1640s, but it was the French Revolution at the end of the eighteenth century and the radical dissent unleashed by that event which gave rise to anarchism as a self-aware tradition rooted in direct action. It was in the nineteenth century and early twentieth that the big guns of anarchism made their appearance – Mikhail Bakunin and Peter Kropotkin most especially, but also individuals like Errico Malatesta and Emma Goldman – while in the late twentieth century many key principles of their thought informed, wittingly and unwittingly, an emerging movement against global capitalism and its philosophical veil of neoliberalism. This movement, as with the Zapatista uprising and the call not only to other Mexicans but to people everywhere to resist economic dictatorship and struggle for self-determination whether they live in the ghettos of India or England, is inseparable from the new anarchism that informed events at Seattle at the end of 1999.

Alongside the political history of anarchism's opposition to the state, there is another dimension to libertarian thought that finds expression in the appeal of anarchist ideas to artists and intellectuals for whom there is something deeply awry with existing forms of representation. Such artists and thinkers seek to deconstruct the hierarchies of their subject areas while at the same time recasting the material in a new, anti-hierarchical key. Chapter Five looks at the ways in which the anarchist impulse has informed or inspired works of literature and the cinema, disciplines like psychology, aesthetics from Dada to Punk and cultural sensibilities like Situationism. The rich variety of alternative epistemologies and aesthetics that emerge from these very diverse fields are not only intrinsically worthwhile but valuable contributions to the viability of thinking and becoming outside of the globalization paradigm. Artists and philosophers creating and thinking in anti-hierarchical ways, yet crucially avoiding the cul-de-sac of postmodernism, can articulate alternative values in ways not unlike those of the anti-capitalist protests that are making themselves heard from first to fourth worlds.

Anarchism cannot ultimately be defined in terms of a political movement, a philosophy or an artistic sensibility. It is all of these and something more, and the tension this creates – the concern of the final chapter – is what makes anarchism so worthwhile and so important.

CHAPTER TWO

Anarchos

State Power

The word anarchy comes from the ancient Greek word ἄναρχος (the letter ν pronounced as *n* in ancient Greek and the letter ρ as *r*), formed from ἀν- ('not') + ἀρχός (leader or chief). The etymology of the word – anarchism meaning the absence of a leader, the absence of a government – signals what is distinctive about anarchism: a rejection of the need for the centralized authority of the unitary state, the only form of government most of us have ever experienced.

The concept of the state is inseparable from the notion of authority within a society. The sovereign state is the source of political authority as we know it, so much so that it is difficult to imagine what political science would be without the concept of the state.[1] The practical manifestation of the state is the government, and it makes little difference to the concept of the state what type of government happens to hold the reins of centralized power, hence the quip that whoever you vote for it is the government that gets in. A distinction that is relevant to the anarchist ideal is the difference between *the government*, referring to the state, and *government*, referring to the administration of a political system. Anarchists, like everyone, tend to use the word government as a

25

synonym for the state, but what is rejected by anarchism's *a priori* opposition to the state is not the concept of government as such but the idea of a sovereign order that claims and demands the obedience, and if necessary the lives, of its subjects. Anarchism rejects the form of imposed, centralized authority enshrined and made material by the state. The anarchist's objection is as animated as it is profound, as Pierre Proudhon, the first to use the term *anarchism* for a political philosophy, makes clear in his oft-quoted denunciation:

> To be GOVERNED is to be at every operation, at every transaction, noted, registered, enrolled, taxed, stamped, measured, numbered, assessed, licensed, authorized, admonished, forbidden, reformed, corrected, punished. It is, under pretext of public utility, and in the name of the general interest, to be placed under contribution, trained, ransomed, exploited, monopolised, extorted, squeezed, mystified, robbed; then, at the slightest resistance, the first word of complaint, to be repressed, fined, despised, harassed, tracked, abused, clubbed, disarmed, choked, imprisoned, judged, condemned, shot, deported, sacrificed, sold, betrayed; and, to crown all, mocked, ridiculed, outraged, dishonoured. That is government; that is justice; that is its morality.[2]

Proudhon's passion for passive verbs throws up a host of different institutions that exercise power but, analytically, the source of the problem lies as much with the idea of the state as a transcendental reality as with its empirical machinery. The state has become accepted as the basis of all and any government, as the single legitimate source of law and violence, and as a body able to claim the obligation of all its subjects. The state has embedded itself within the concept of the nation, giving it both a rhetorical and a seemingly natural claim on our allegiance. The political authority of one state is essentially no different from that of other states, and yet each state differentiates itself from the other because of its fused identity with the nation.

The extreme case of state power is the outbreak of war, when a remarkably small number of people in charge of governments make decisions claiming the lives of millions and then announce it on television as a *fait accompli*. No referendums are held, and governments making such decisions, in states where there are general elections, do not have previously published manifestos with a commitment to go to war if they see fit. This is all in the small print, for when a government is in power it has the authority to declare war and, if deemed necessary, make unconditional claims on the active participation of every adult citizen. Governments, like the Allied states in the world war of 1939–45 that took some 85 million lives, usually claim moral justification for their wars and, equally usually, such claims are bogus. Defeating Nazism was morally justifiable, but ethics is not a cheque that can be backdated, and some of the causes of that war – the willingness of a German capitalist state to embrace an anti-communist Hitler and the toleration of this by other states, and in the Pacific the aggressive and oppressive containment of Japan by the US – were created by the attitudes and policies of those same Allied governments in Europe and Asia prior to 1939. The strongest case to which ethics could apply, that of opposing the genocidal racism of Nazism, was not in any sense a motive or even a contributory cause in the Allies' decisions to go to war and conduct it in the way they did. An individual could choose to oppose Fascism by going to war against Nazi Germany and feel morally vindicated in doing so, but it was, and remains, hypocritical for the Allied states to make such a claim. It might be thought that the horrors of twentieth-century wars are more a revelation of flaws in human nature than an argument about state power, but the two world wars are inseparable from the governments that brought them into being. It was governments, acting in ways that they thought represented their best interests, that led up to the outbreak of World War II, and notwithstanding that war's complexities, and the fact that defeating Nazism was laudable, World War II was as much a struggle for power between national states as was World War I, and it was on this basis that capable citizens of those states were conscripted to fight and die on a massive scale.

The modern state's ability to conscript citizens has always relied more on the voluntary loyalty of patriotism than any enforced militarization, and it is possibly more difficult today than ever before for governments to take this patriotism for granted. This is not due to any weakening of state power – the technology of surveillance, for example, has increased the power of state institutions – but it does suggest a weakening of ideological control over citizens when it comes to conventional warfare. Sophisticated modern states, however, are not so likely to try and recruit large armies of men in the pursuit of economic control over smaller nations. Colonization, backed up by military coercion, has been replaced by peaceful economic neo-colonization under the guise of globalization – though always with the option of resorting to war where circumstances are thought to demand it.

The relative peace that Western societies have enjoyed since 1945 tends to blur acknowledgement of the fact that states, including liberal democracies, can involve their citizens, and not just their armed forces, in a state of war. It is equally easy to forget that a state that feels threatened will kill its own citizens in an attempt to assert control. The events of Bloody Sunday in 1972, when fourteen civilians were killed on the streets of a city in Northern Ireland, is an example of this: for although some individual soldiers may simply have run amok on the day, the British authorities were growing increasingly intolerant of Free Derry, an enclave of the city that had effectively withdrawn from the body politic, and this refusal by the citizens of Free Derry to accept the authority of the state led to the dispatch of the Parachute Regiment to the city. The situation in Northern Ireland was unique, but, while it is unusual for a modern European state to kill its own citizens, the response of the British state was not unique, and it is not difficult to list instances of modern states killing their citizens in public, from the campus of an American state university to the central square of China's capital city and, more recently, the shooting dead of Carlo Giuliani on the streets of Genoa in July 2001 during protests against a G8 summit. Indeed, the ferocity of the police violence at Genoa, its degree of premeditation and the level of political support from the Italian government that lay behind it clearly shows how the state is prepared to deal with the threat of effectively organized dissent by its own citizens, even when this dissent is broadly fuelled by peaceful protestors. This may seem like an extreme view to some, but Indymedia's *Genoa Red Zone* video[3] shows the reasonableness of just such an interpretation of what happened in the Italian city.

Anarchism rejects the state as a form of government for specific reasons. The adage about power corrupting and absolute power corrupting absolutely is taken to heart by anarchists, and for good reason. Whether it be a Stalinist state with its gulags or a US under corporate control (which in respect of blighting the lives of one section of society on a systematic scale has its own version of Stalin's gulags: nearly 10 per cent of blacks between the ages of 25 and 29, as compared with 1.1 per cent of whites, serve time in prison[4]), anarchism builds from the premise that any system of government is flawed if power is centralized and unaccountable. In the case of an imposed dictatorship such a premise seems perfectly sensible, but anarchists regard the ability of one elite class to exert economic and social control over a 'democratic' society as another form of unaccountable power. Rejecting the view that the state is the only alternative to lawless barbarism, anarchists regard the political machinery of liberal democracies as a sophisticated cover for what would otherwise be revealed as nasty and brutal self-interest. It does not follow from this that anarchists would regard living in a liberal democracy as no better than living under a crude dictatorship. This is far from the case, and in this respect anarchists can appreciate the virtues of liberal democracies as much as any political conservative. In times of crisis, though, the liberal, fragile veneer wears dangerously and revealingly thin. In the United States in the wake of September 11, for example, the detention of thousands of civilians without trial and what effectively amounted to a government Press as regards reporting news of this, blurred the distinction between a 'free Press' and the old Soviet Pravda.[5] The standard objection to an example like this, as it is to incidents such as Bloody Sunday, is that organized violence against the state produces an understandable and, in principle if not always in particular cases, a justifiable willingness on the part of the state to defend itself in ways that would not normally be countenanced in a liberal political order. Society, so the argument goes, is predicated on everyone agreeing to certain basic liberal rules, and if these are breached then the state has no option but to reply in kind. Anarchists reply that this is only a clever excuse to disguise the fact that modern states will, and do, resort to brute force to protect the sectional interests of those they represent, and that the liberal rules function as little more than a sophisticated cloaking device for a ruling class to maintain power. A state, far from requiring the provocation of organized violence being directed against it, will reveal its own brute nature whenever a crisis threatens the interests of those that it exists to serve. Power, like love, is put to the test in times of crisis, and to support their argument anarchists can point to many examples of modern states being prepared to use its police, its armed forces, even initiate wars, against essentially peaceful but effectively organized movements that threaten the ruling class. The use of the British army against striking miners in the 1920s, the US government actively intervening to depose an elected government in Guatemala in 1954 or the democratically elected government of Chile in 1973, the use of the British police to prevent striking miners reaching Kent coalfields to picket them during the 1984–5 miners' strike are only some of the more blatant instances of this. What distinguishes anarchists from traditional communists is that they apply a very similar analysis to non-capitalist states and point to events in Russia shortly after 1917 as an example of this.

The power of centralized government in liberal democracies is regarded by anarchists as unaccountable despite universal suffrage. Putting a cross on a piece of paper every few years, and accepting whatever new laws and obligations are enacted in that period, can be seen as a neat example of how power is preserved under the guise of democracy. Anarchists are not alone in rejecting the ballot box as a spurious form of democracy: 60 per cent of people between the age of 18 and 24 did not vote in the UK 2001 general election and only 52 per cent of American voters participated in the US 2000 presidential election.[6] Such non-votes do not count politically, of course, and even a government elected on less than 50 per cent of the total vote (never mind that governments are rarely put into power by more than half the voting electorate) still constitutes a legitimate government. It is not unusual for anarchists to use voting figures in their arguments because, while democracy teaches the virtues of representative government, the figures are evidence of the fact that a large percentage of citizens chooses not to vote for any of their would-be representatives. This does not make non-voters into anarchists, but the resigned shrug behind the 'whoever you vote for, the government gets in' attitude, even the lazy reasoning that an individual vote won't make any difference so really I needn't go to the trouble of voting, does nevertheless suggest widespread dissatisfaction and/or cynicism with the functioning of 'democracy'. The dissatisfaction is there, despite the media's constant creation of political news that helps sustain an image of a healthy body politic. Politicians mingle occasionally with small sections of the public, usually when there is an election, but for most of the time there is a fraught gulf between many people and the system of representative government to which they supposedly subscribe. Anarchists usually champion non-voting as a means of expressing a political choice, albeit it the negative one of rejecting all of the candidates, but the principle of chosen representatives – probationary, accountable and replaceable – is far from anathema to anarchists. The act of not-voting is not a cardinal principle of anarchism, written in stone.

Nor should it be thought that anarchists necessarily relish, as an end itself, the prospect of more and more people choosing not to vote. It could be envisaged that at some stage it might make sense to try and build on the indifference or hostility of voters towards existing candidates and use it as a basis for direct action, as, in a very different context, a majority of Irish voters chose to do when casting their ballots in 1918 (and as they continue to do in a number of constituencies in Northern Ireland) in order to elect representatives in the full knowledge that the successful candidates would refuse to take up their seats.

A Revolution to Dance To

Underlying anarchism's objections to the consequences of state power lies an equally fundamental libertarian principle, one that sees the need to challenge many notions of authority and obedience. The force of this principle often finds expression in non-political forms, especially in the aesthetic sphere and in the rejection of the kind of social constraints and hierarchical structures – particularly psychological forms of coercion and gender conditioning – that led to Emma Goldman's insistence that she did not want a revolution that she couldn't dance to. This is the concern of chapter Five, but its broader delineation informs the wide arc of the anarchist movement in its philosophical, political and cultural forms.

State power is a material force that, most of the time, has to be accepted as a fact of life in the sense that alternative activity has a habit of landing dissidents in a court of law. This kind of power in the form of courts, prisons, nuclear missiles and so on, is a brute fact that we have to live with whatever our private feelings, but thinking that we should accept authority is deeply ingrained in our social and political life and it can be surprisingly difficult to question. The idea of submitting to authority is something inside our heads, something difficult to think outside of.

Accepting authority in this context should be distinguished from accepting professional opinion and judgement; anarchists are not objecting to some people having a more authoritative voice than others in fields where this is appropriate. In aspects of child-rearing or medicine, for example, or in particular fields of science, anarchists can see the reasonableness of exercising or accepting authority. This would be a moral choice or judgement, based on reason. Bakunin spelled out what is at stake:

> Does it follow that I reject all authority? Far from me such a thought. In the matter of boots, I refer to the bootmaker; concerning houses, canals or railroads, I consult the architect or the engineer . . . But I allow neither the bootmaker nor the architect . . . to impose his authority upon me. I listen to them freely and with all the respect merited [but] . . . I have no absolute faith in any person. Such a faith would be fatal to my reason, to my liberty, and even to the success of my undertakings; it would immediately transform me into a stupid slave, an instrument of the will and interests of others.[7]

The import of Bakunin's remarks has been borne out in a famous set of experiments, whereby a random number of people accepted instructions to inflict what they were led to believe were increasingly dangerous levels of electric shock on subjects, who duly simulated agonizing cries of torment.[8] Those following the instructions did not know the pain was simulated, and yet many of them obeyed the orders to continue increasing the voltage. For Alex Comfort, anarchist polymath and author of *The Joy of Sex*, disobedience is a moral imperative in the face of irresponsible state power: 'Resistance and disobedience are still the only forces able to cope with barbarism, and so long as we do not practise them we are unarmed.'[9] The conduct of the Allies in World War II – especially the firebombing of German cities and the mass slaughter of their citizens – was the kind of barbarism that made Comfort a pacifist. Oscar Wilde, whose theatricality has tended to disguise his libertarian socialism and his sense of history, similarly emphasized the importance of rebellion:

> Disobedience, in the eyes of anyone who has read history, is man's original virtue. It is through disobedience that progress has been made, through disobedience and through rebellion.[10]

The liberal conscience, of course, feeds off stories like Wilde's arrest, imprisonment and premature death by safely situating his fate in an age of *fin de siècle* unenlightenment. His rebelliousness is elevated to iconoclasm or a stylish pose, so that talk of disobedience and insubordination remains something naïve, unsophisticated, adolescent. All too familiar is the portrayal of anarchists as youthful but dangerous rebels who, once they gain some experience and maturity, will see the recklessness of their youthful idealism and become more like everyone else. Becoming more like other people is exactly what Wilde the anarchist opposed. Utopia, the land that he said every map should allow for, was for Wilde a place without government and without private property, a state of mind as much as a state of the economy, where the personality expresses its individuality of being. The purpose of life – *being* – is not based on an imaginary notion of psychic unity, and Wilde spurned the falsity of the romantic notion of sincerity. What mattered was the avoidance of shallowness and the pursuit of authenticity in all its androgynous plurality.

In *The Soul of Man Under Socialism*, Wilde pointedly expressed the anarchist ideal by weaving together the sometimes contrary claims of socialism and the spirit of the free individual, recognizing a difference between individualization and individualism (as Kropotkin would do in his article on anarchism in the eleventh edition of the *Encyclopaedia Britannica*).[11] Dispensing with terms like the worker or the producer, Wilde wrote instead of the freeing of the personality in a socialist community that accords every individual the freedom that the artist so ardently requires. He sees that only the abolition of private property will free people from the fetish of owning and having and allow them, instead, to be. Wilde is sometimes thought of as a champagne socialist, but this is a misplaced criticism and there is little that is wishy-washy about his libertarian socialism; it is rooted in individualization but dependent on communism and accompanied by a fine sense of social realism. Like Bakunin, he prophetically warned of the dangers of an authoritarian left-wing state; and like Bakunin also, he championed the dispossessed and the marginalized who refused to be cowed. Such groups may not be politically aware, but their discontent makes them intelligent, as does their refusal to be taken in by the charity of do-gooders. The 'virtuous poor', dutiful, tabloid-reading and conformist, 'have made private terms with the enemy, and sold their birthright for very bad pottage'.[12] Though acutely aware of what material poverty does to people, Wilde was equally conscious of the poverty of thought that cuts across social class. This poverty, he saw, is caused by the nature of authority that, whether from a dictatorship or a democracy, robs people of the dignity everyone is capable of. Whatever its source and means, authority tends to bribe people to conform so that, often without realizing it, the clothes they wear and the opinions they share are in effect second-hand; they are like petted animals.

Wilde's art and politics merge on the stage where his dramas constantly play with identities, role reversals and dichotomies of gender. Wilde's seditious hijacking of English literary forms was conveniently underplayed by forgetting his Irishness and his own historical identity as a colonial subject. His dramas may seem merely to play with social forms along the lines of Buñuel's *The Discreet Charm of the Bourgeoisie*, but they carry a subversive message, undermining the posing that occasions so many identities. This is enacted by dramatizing on stage the wafer-thin personas of the bourgeoisie; and doing so with such poise and polish that middle-class audiences would identify with and envy what is really the subject of ridicule. Wilde's scorn was especially directed at middle-class mores, but his subversive thrust comes from dramatizing the realization that identities so socially constructed are really ungrounded, and just as capable of being unmade as made.

Wilde's deconstruction of the subject raises questions about the nature of human beings and, in particular, the level of meaning given to the concept of human nature. For some anarchist thinkers, such as Noam Chomsky, there is a human nature in the sense of innate, bio-physical schematics that underlies the mind (while his work as a linguist has concerned itself with discovering the foundational structures of human language Chomsky, interestingly, does not draw any strict inferences or parallels between his scientific work and his political philosophy), but on the whole anarchism does not attach too much significance to abstract questions about human nature and prefers an ontology that largely relocates the idea and substance of human nature in the landscape of an essentially changeable reality. Anarchists tend to follow Marx in thinking of human nature not as fixed and immutable but as something that is largely governed by dynamic human activity of a social and economic nature. The philosophical idea that reality is a changeable feast rather than a fixed event in the human calendar is a core belief for many anarchists, and thus claims to universal truths like human nature are suspect notions. This topic is a focus of the following chapter because of its philosophical relevance to anarchism, namely the significance that is attached to the idea that often we are who we are because of the way of life we live, what Wittgenstein calls 'forms of life', and if ways of living are changed then a people's nature will change as well. This is the anarchist's response to the familiar refrain that libertarian communism might sound like a beautiful idea but is doomed to failure because of certain unpalatable truths about human nature.

Anarchism is also suspicious about claims to universal truths, especially notions of a fixed human nature, because history shows how such ideas, while seeming to be politically neutral, are in fact bound up with issues of power and control. In this area of thought, Michel Foucault's work is relevant. His investigations into history show how claims to knowledge are imbricated with hierarchies of power and domination, and this can be allied to anarchism even though Foucault himself was reluctant to identify himself with any system of thought *per se*. This is partly the result of a methodological imperative on his part that rejects any 'ism', preferring to characterize himself as a historian of ideas, especially the idea of human subjectivity. The way in which human beings are made into subjects, and made to see themselves as those subjects, is an historical process, and in books like *Madness and Civilization, The History of Sexuality* and *Discipline and Punishment*, Foucault famously studied the ways in which certain social groups are objectified and marginalized by the discourses of more powerful groups. His work is important to anarchism because of the way his historical studies explore how the totality of the state developed and how state power has grown to invade areas of life that once were beyond its concern. The post-Renaissance state began to extend the parameters of its power beyond the traditional domain of the territorial and into what we still like to think of as the private realm.

Foucault's best-known example of disciplinary technology is the Panopticon, a special prison planned by Jeremy Bentham, the nineteenth-century social reformer and jurist. From a tower in the prison it would be possible to observe every cell, but with the inmates never knowing when they are under active surveillance. The Panopticon, a paradigm of surveillance that allowed for total control of the body but which was conceived of as utterly rational and utilitarian, showed how rationality is conscripted into a process of control and domination. It seemed reasonable to Bentham to introduce the idea of the Panopticon to his readers, and in our world today we are increasingly led to think it reasonable that the bureaucratic and institutional practises behind Proudhon's catalogue of verbs, far from being based on a histrionic list of impositions and intrusions, are normal hallmarks of a modern society. Proudhon's list, indeed, invites an extension that allows for more recent techniques of control: videotaped, camcorded, monitored, supervised, documented, classified, itemized, passworded, photographed, authorized, digitized, bar-coded, categorized, National Curriculum-ized, discount-carded, reward-carded, systematized, DNA-ed, CCTV-ed,[13] access-control carded, ID-carded, data-based, census-tagged, measured, assessed, serialized, scanned, spun, appraised, hierarchized, objectified. When these are added to Proudhon's list, the litany may begin to sound paranoid, but when the terms are taken separately they can all be interpreted as rational, discreet aspects of a modern state to which no normal citizen would usually object. This is not to suggest that life in a modern liberal state is really no different to living under an Orwellian-style dictatorship. On the contrary, as Foucault was concerned to show, a distinguishing aspect of the way power can function is in the internalization of compliant roles that may lead to submissive self-policing on the part of the subject citizen. The concept of normality is highly suspect to anarchists and they would accept Foucault's advice, as would have Wilde, that 'maybe the target nowadays is not to discover what we are, but to refuse what we are'.[14] What we are, Foucault is saying, can mean being conformist and submissive, accepting the social and political identities that we happen to inherit historically as if they were natural and unchangeable.

The Anarchist Spectrum

Politically, anarchism's rejection of state power may be delineated in terms of an arc that spans communism and extreme individualism. It is a broad arc, ecumenical by nature and with blurred peripheries, but there are some clearly definable boundaries, as well as some confused positions lurking in the shadows of the boundaries.

One boundary is reached where communist anarchism parts company with traditional communism, most crucially over the role of the state and methods of organizing resistance to the *status quo*. Another equally important boundary is reached when individualist anarchism becomes indistinguishable from extreme right-wing conservatism and its worship of the free market. The term 'anarcho-capitalism' for this domain of right-wing libertarianism is generally regarded as a political oxymoron by anarchists, but it points to an ambiguity about libertarianism that won't go away.

Black is the colour traditionally associated with anarchism, with black and red flags often espoused by anarchist groups as a mark of their allegiance to the twin ideals of anarchism and communism. At the other end of the spectrum is individualist anarchism. The extreme individualist camp, sometimes more eager about espousing the virtues of raw capitalism than anarchism, possesses an essentially conservative agenda. This is suggested by the difficulty right-wing free marketeers have in extending the liberty of the market-place to complete freedom in other areas like those of lifestyle and sexual preferences. Right-wing advocates of the free market use the language of libertarianism but tend to restrict libertarian principles to the economic sphere: commodities must be free to circulate without hindrance by the state, but not, for instance, sexual identities.

Individualist anarchism pushes the classical liberal position and its vocabulary of freedom, justice, tolerance and individual rights to the point of no return as far as the state is concerned. One of the most eloquent expressions of liberalism is John Rawls's *A Theory of Justice* (1971), with its notion of a social contract between a free person and a minimal, 'nightwatchman's' state. *A Theory of Justice* provides a philosophical foundation for the welfare state, carefully reasoning from libertarian principles why legislation is needed to ensure equal opportunities to all. A colleague of Rawls, Robert Nozick, replied in 1974 with *Anarchy, State, and Utopia*, arguing the need for a far more minimal state than anything proposed by

Rawls, and the purest possible free market. Supporters of this kind of free and stateless society, envisioned most characteristically by theorists in the US, arrive at various solutions to the challenge of explaining how a stateless society could provide essential public services. Utopia becomes a community where property enjoys the same inviolable rights as the sovereign individual, and law courts and essential services like those of policing are provided by private agencies. Such agencies, created by the free market, would contract their services to individuals or community groups. The overall emphasis tends to be on the negative side – insisting on what is not the province of government and what should not be done to one individual by groups of other individuals.

The fervour with which the free-market American right took up Nozick's thesis in the 1970s and '80s shows that when individualist anarchism becomes part of the argument for right-wing, *laissez faire* economics, it has little in common with mainstream anarchism. The social libertarianism of Nozick's argument, which included such issues as the legalisation of prostitution and drugs, did not impress the American right or those more moved by a philosophy that would endorse inalienable property rights. The fact that arguments of a libertarian kind can be used in support of raw capitalism and in invocation of the freedom of the property-owning individual against the power of the interfering state, reflects the elasticity in the concept of freedom: freedom can be invoked to support the freedom to be selfish. However, a continuum does exist within anarchism between individualism and communism, and a consequence of this is that different libertarians can emphasize one at the expense of the other. While nineteenth-century anarchists like Kropotkin, and contemporary voices like that of Murray Bookchin, are models of communist anarchism, Max Stirner (1806–56) remains the exemplary advocate of individualist anarchism. Part of an historical understanding of the appeal of modern individualist anarchism in the US lies in its intellectual roots, and these roots were nurtured and influenced by the German Max Stirner and his resounding and uncompromising declaration of individualism in *The Ego and Its Own* (1844–5).

According to Part 1 of *The Ego and Its Own*, God is dead, but not Christian morality, and the notion of 'the other world' continues to blight us with ideas of some human essence that lays a claim on us, just as principles of human rights blight by telling us who we are. Consequently, Stirner argues, an internalized, psychic authority continues to bedevil our autonomy. He champions egoism as the means to enjoy and expand life, cultivating one's own welfare and loving humanity, for example, because you want to and not because you ought:

Freedom teaches only: Get yourselves rid, relieve yourself of everything burdensome; it does not teach you who you yourselves are. Rid, rid! That is its battlecry, get rid even of yourselves, it says 'deny yourself'. But ownness calls you back to yourselves, it says 'come to yourself!' [15]

Stirner's blistering attack on the state in Part 2 of *The Ego and Its Own* is bound up with his existential notion of 'ownness'. The notion has an obvious appeal to anarchists insofar as 'ownness' represents the inviolable right of every individual to enjoy to the full the opportunities that society offers for self-expression, self-discovery and self-invention. Stirner is also concerned with the way certain ideas of knowledge aspire to truths and how a group or class can claim, on the basis of having access to this realm of knowledge, a special status. This, in turn, paves the way for a hierarchical division within society, one that distinguishes those with knowledge from those without. Knowledge, he asserts, is part of a continuum grounded in individual experience, the here and now, and not some realm of pure knowledge and metaphysical nonsense. What Stirner has to say about claims to special knowledge being used as a basis for the creation of an elite seem applicable to the emergence of the world's first states. It is likely that ancient Mesopotamia first saw a development of this kind, facilitating the earliest creation of class divisions through a family group that could claim a unique relationship with the gods and, by relying on a surplus production of food, establish a special class of priests that could avoid having to labour.

Max Stirner, nihilist and crude harbinger of Nietzsche, remains a disturbing thinker for many anarchists. While warming to his attacks on the state and his celebration of the power of the individual – the very aspects that made Stirner attractive to American thinkers – many anarchists draw back from the implications of his extreme individualism. The reason for this is that they share the concerns that provoked Karl Marx, Stirner's contemporary, into devoting hundreds of pages in *The German Ideology* to rebutting his arguments. Marx recoiled at the asocial and ahistorical implications of Stirner's individualism, and many anarchists, for much the same reason, like to take their Stirner in small shots because of the perils of an overdose. Stirner's notion of 'owness' is a long way from anarchism's traditional emphasis on communal direct action, fellowship and mutual aid as a response to the injustices of capitalism. The existential self, which is what 'owness' refers to, ignores the way in which the self is created by material and historical circumstances. The existential consciousness does not exist in a social vacuum, and to regard the individual purely as an individual is to disregard the social forces that help shape our understanding of what it means to be an individual in the first place.

In this sense, then, Stirnerism is far removed from mainstream communist anarchism. The communist heart of anarchism views freedom in the way that Wilde conceives of it, anchored in a social being that celebrates individualization. When cut adrift from its social anchor the value of freedom, understood as pure individualism and experienced as such, tends to lapse into what Murray Bookchin calls lifestyle anarchism. Bookchin, a senior American voice of anarchism, is driven at times to splenetic attacks on individualist anarchism, perhaps because he is able to observe at close quarters the way in which the US nurtures lifestyle libertarianism at the expense of radical, down-to-earth politics.[16] Unfortunately, such attacks lead to Bookchin unceremoniously lumping together individualist anarchism with New Age and Yippie-like ideas of personal enlightenment, all stirred into a hotchpotch with primitivism and bits of postmodernism. In the process, Stirner, Nietzsche and Foucault are tarred with the same brush that more correctly colours antics like California-style psychotherapy as the narcissistic affairs they usually are. Bookchin's blanket labelling, which castigates variously different radical ideas as comparable aspects of bourgeois decadence, has a habit of obscuring finer value judgements that could be made. More usefully, though, he situates the deracinated anarchism that underpins lifestyle libertarianism as a symptom of powerlessness under modern capitalism, and his truculent criticisms are more focused when it comes to assessing the worth of primitivism in relation to anarchism. Primitivism, a particular brand of American anti-authoritarianism that claims to be anarchist but which, like anarcho-capitalism, has a more natural home on the individualist fringes of right-wing extremism, came to public attention in the events surrounding the hunt for the Unabomber in the 1990s.

Ted Kaczynski, who resigned from a university teaching post in 1967, had retreated to a 10 x 12-feet cabin in Montana, without electricity or running water, living there until he was arrested in 1996 for a spate of bombings that had begun in the late 1970s. The *Washington Post* and the *New York Times* had published the Unabomber's manifesto, which provided the rationale for such attacks, in return for a promise to end the bombings. The attacks did end but Kaczynski was arrested the following year.

Kaczynski was influenced by the writings of primitivists like John Zerzan, whose texts locate the ills of civilization in civilization itself and the malign effects occasioned by its worship of technology. For primitivism, technology *in itself*, rather than corporate technology driven by the market need for profit, becomes a force that structures our way of living by replicating its rigid, alien forms in social reality. Technology has not only gone beyond the control of its creator and, like Frankenstein's monster, assumed a life of its own, it has also acquired an ontological force. Primitivism opposes the monster of machinery with a vision of the primal Palaeolithic, a world that was 'affluent because its needs are few, all its desires are easily met. Its tool kit is elegant and light-weight . . . It is anarchic . . . a dancing society, a singing society, a celebrating society, a dreaming society.'[17] Some primitive societies can indeed be appreciated in terms of their non-authoritarian, non-statist character, but primitivism often invites derision because of foolish generalizations that present a diagrammatic and atemporal dichotomy between primitive bliss and totalitarian technology. Even at its most sophisticated, as when defining technology in such a way as not to preclude primitivism's own use of modern technology, primitivism lacks a sense of how the use of technology is related to the demands of capitalism. For example, the peaceful and non-statist society of the forest-dwelling Penan in the Malaysian state of Sarawak was destroyed in the late 1980s as giant machines literally cut down their habitat. But the chain-saw technology that destroyed their home and culture was a function of timber companies seeking to maximize profits with the assistance of a compliant government.[18] It was the profit motive not the megamachine that despoiled the Penan way of life, and making sense of what happened to the Penan, and drawing a lesson from their plight, brings together history, economics and politics in a way that has little in common with the ahistorical outlook of many primitivists. Anyone dipping into primitivism on the web[19] or in the *Green Anarchist* will find texts from the likes of Adorno and Horkheimer conscripted to the cause, but the cause cannot sustain such heavyweights because it lacks their complex, Marxist sense of history. Similarly, the paucity of primitivism is only revealed by placing its anthropology alongside Nietzsche's searing insights in *On the Genealogy of Morals*, or primitivism's attack on technology alongside Heidegger's essay on the subject.[20]

The weakness of primitivism is reflected in the humdrum prose of the Unabomber's Manifesto. The opening statement combines reasonable observations with a frailty of historical analysis that is fairly typical of the confusion of thought characterizing primitivism.

The Industrial Revolution and its consequences have been a disaster for the human race. They have greatly increased the life-expectancy of those of us who live in 'advanced' countries, but they have destabilized society, have made life unfulfilling, have subjected human beings to indignities, have led to widespread psychological suffering (in the Third World to physical suffering as well) and have inflicted severe damage on the natural world.[21]

What is here identified as the Industrial Revolution or, in the next paragraph of the manifesto, 'the industrial-technological system', is a roundabout name for modern capitalism, but the failure to recognize this means the way is not open for an historical understanding. Instead, expressing a basic tenet of primitivism, the root cause of our social ills becomes anthropological in origin. Industrialization is seen to be profoundly at odds with the way human beings have evolved to behave, robbing humanity of the dignity and autonomy that is essential for the attainment of goals. Technology, by forcing the pace and nature of change, causes a rupture in what it means to be human, and the result is a paralyz-ing sense of insecurity that disables people's ability to be happy and content. The Manifesto argues that the individual freedoms accorded to citizens are perfunctory because they are not the important ones and there-fore fail to address people's need for meaningful fulfilment. What makes such accounts seem like little more than high-school sociology is attribut-able to the poverty of analysis that primitivism lays claim to. This is not to mock the validity of Kaczynski's dissent from, and hatred of, the system he opposes, any more than it belittles the fact that three people lost their lives as a result of the Unabomber's actions, but the point is that primitivism makes only a marginal contribution to anarchism, as this book understands the term.

Kropotkin, whose five years travelling in eastern Siberia and northern Manchuria brought him into direct contact with a number of primitive lifeways, provides a return to the black and red colours of anarchism. Kropotkin, hearing 'the shriek of the engine . . . in the wild gorges of the Alps, the Caucasus and the Himalayas', saw for himself the positive force of 'all those iron slaves we call machines'. Kropotkin, seeing how technology was bound up with social and economic life, drew a moral from the realization that the development of steam power would not have taken the form it did if James Watt at Soho, Birmingham, had not found

> skilled workmen to embody his ideas in metal, bringing all the parts of his engine to perfection, so that steam, pent in a complete mechanism, and rendered more docile than a horse, more manageable than water, became at last the very soul of modern industry. Every machine has had the same history . . . of disillusions and of joys, of partial improvements discovered by several generations of nameless workers . . . By what right then can any one whatever appropriate the least morsel of this immense whole and say – This is mine, not yours?[22]

Anarchists oppose capitalism for much the same reasons as socialists do. The capitalist economic system is viewed as necessarily unfair, privileging power in the hands of a discrete class at the expense of ordinary working people. Anarchism parts company with state socialism when it comes to preparing the way for an alternative to the capitalist system. In a socialist or communist state, notwithstanding its commitment to justice and equality, power is still vested in the state. The main difference is that such a socialist state claims to represent an alternative system to capitalism. Anarchists argue that states embody authoritarian power structures in their very form, structures that are inimical to the non-hierarchical nature of communism, and that a communist society would no more have a centralized government than the Vatican would have a woman as Pope.

Who Empties the Privies?

Anthropologists have recorded numerous examples of stateless societies functioning around the world, from hunter-gatherers to Berbers.[23] While this comes as no great surprise for many people, it fails as an argument for the viability of anarchism in the twentieth-first century. Forest-dwelling Penans may manage an anarchic existence, or at least they did until the Malaysian government dragooned them into statehood in the 1980s and '90s, but most people have difficulty in relating anthropological case histories to modern urban life. Examples of mass anarchist action, as in Cuba in the 1920s when 80,000 to 100,000 workers, out of a total population of under three million, built one of the largest anarcho-syndicalist movements in the world,[24] or the remarkable events in Spain a decade later, are not well known about, but even if they were there would be a tendency to see them as belonging to a different, less complicated world. Modern life, and the material expectations that accompany it, is seen as just too complex for anarchism to handle. Hence the Pavlovian response that rhetorically asks Who, when all is said and done, will clean public toilets, keep hooligans at bay and supermarket shelves stocked with cheap wine?[25]

A large part of the difficulty is the wholesale acceptance of the idea that the absence of centralized government and state power means the absence of *any* kind of government and order. Anarchism is not so barking mad as to think the complexities of modern life can be managed without organization and planning, sometimes requiring centralized order at national and international levels. Anarchism naturally recognizes that many indispensable and useful activities are carried out by governments. What is opposed is the idea that government can only function in terms of the centralized state: anarchism insists on autonomy and self-government because of the knowledge that new governments – even radical socialist ones – will only replicate the already existing hierarchical power structures. Government for anarchists takes the forms, instead, of the kind of social agencies and organizations that already exist, including complex and sophisticated ones, that structure their identity on non-exploitative rules and values of social solidarity. The anarchist Errico Malatesta (1853–1932) observed how a large part of what we consider most important in life takes place within structures not linked to government:

> Men work, barter, study, travel and follow to the best of their knowledge moral rules and those of well-being; they benefit from the advances made in science and the arts, have widespread relations among themselves – all without feeling the need for somebody to tell them how to behave. Indeed, it is just those matters over which government has no control that work best . . . [26]

And, writing in 1891, he pointed to the Red Cross, geographical societies, workers' associations and voluntary bodies as examples of the power of the spirit of cooperation.[27] Anarchism seeks to create government in terms of voluntary associations, forms of federalism, functionally specific organizations and directly accountable representatives; dis-organization is not the same as disorganization. Similar principles would govern the complex tasks of production and distribution requiring coordinated activity at a national or international level.

While so-called anarcho-capitalism would embrace the free market as its economic model, mainstream anarchism seeks to replace the competitive market with a communal system of production and distribution based on needs and availability rather than on demand and supply. It is not a matter of just an economy but an economy that is just. Establishing the means and methods of running and coordinating a communist economy without recourse to Soviet-style centralized planning and control would be the defining task for any communist society based on libertarian principles. A lot of economic planning would be on a participatory and local scale, with national and international planning for complex modes of production and scarce or locally unavailable resources. For anarchism to work in a modern industrial world, means must be developed to replace essential services presently managed by the state or private monopolies. The central organizational idea proposed by anarchists is that of the federation, built up from a democratic base of associations, councils and communes, arriving at joint decisions and exercizing authority but in a way that does not recreate the authoritarian rule of the state. From Bolshevism to Blairism, twentieth-century history provides many examples of left-wing parties gaining supreme power, using the existing machinery of state to effect economic and social change, only eventually to resemble too much the form of government they sought to replace. By organizing and working on libertarian principles, federalism seeks a workable alternative that will not end up replicating existing relations of authority and obedience. How such a programme might work in practice, and the kind of tension points that could emerge, have been tackled by anarchist theorists in various ways.

Anarchism has been saddled with an undeserved *naïveté* for a variety of reasons, one of which is based on its perceived failure to address the issue of political power. This is particularly erroneous in one way because the organization of power is part of the core of the anarchist project. It is because power is so undeniably a human drive that anarchism places its diffusion through decentralization at the heart of its practice. This is a way of dealing with it, not a way of abolishing it, and even then it is frankly acknowledged that power will tend to re-emerge in other forms. It doesn't require the research papers of anthropologists to make the point that patriarchy, religion, leaders, gerontocracy and the power of conformity are capable of surviving without the formal apparatus of the state. A beneficial side-effect of states enjoying a monopoly over the legitimate use of violence, especially in well-run liberal democracies, is that public peace tends to be preserved. Only the most utopian of anarchists would resist admitting that, in the absence of a perfect society, there will be a need for sanctions, even coercion, along the way to a better society. The power of sanctions, in psychological, social or legal ways, will operate however diffuse the structure of power relationships. For while centralized governments tend to hold a monopoly over legal sanctions, the replacement of such governments by voluntary cooperatives would not eliminate the need for sanctions, nor would it remove the possibility of familiar aspects of authority and control emerging in disguised forms. Ursula Le Guin confronts this fact in her finely imagined science-fiction novel *The Dispossessed* (1974).

Imagining the Real

One of the reasons that makes Le Guin's *The Dispossessed* such a successful endeavour to imagine an anarchist society is her willingness to explore the problems and tensions that could develop in such an alternative community. Shevek, on a mission to Urras from the anarchist world of Anarres, becomes a pre-Gorbachev type of character who tries to preserve his society's essential principles while striving to combat a dispiriting malaise that has developed on the moon world of Anarres. On Anarres, created seven generations earlier when anarchist dissidents from Urras agreed to exile themselves, human nature may be different in a number of fundamental ways, but this does not mean that emotions like jealousy and xenophobia have ceased to exist. Within the syndicates on Anarres that deal with administrative affairs on a national level, informal hierarchies have developed, and being informal they are all the more difficult to identify and contest. Shevek, originator of a secret theoretical physics that will revolutionize space travel, has to contend with a conformist mindset and authoritarian impulses that have re-emerged in his society. He comes up against such reactionary tendencies in individuals like Sabul, an older physicist who pays lip service to libertarian ideals but who has learned to use the system to stifle creativity. A friend of Shevek's sees what has happened:

> You can't crush ideas by suppressing them. You can only crush them by ignoring them. By refusing to think – refusing to change. And that's precisely what our society is doing! Sabul uses you where he can, and where he can't, he prevents you from publishing, from teaching, even from working. Right? In other words, he has power over you. Where does he get it from? Not from vested authority, there isn't any. Not from intellectual excellence, he hasn't any. He gets it from the cowardice of the average human mind. Public opinion! That's the power structure he's part of, and knows how to use.[28]

While intelligently probing such problems, *The Dispossessed* creates a credible picture of a functioning anarchist society. Le Guin wryly draws out the gaps in language and thought that divide the use-value consciousness of the physicist Shevek from those of the people he meets on the exchange-value world of Urras. Methods of organizing work, the nature of government, the role of art and education, sexual attitudes and the existence of violence in an anarchist society are dealt with, not brushed over or dispersed in woolly metaphors. Embodying some of the ideas advanced by Kropotkin, citizens work in exchange for the necessities of life. There is no need for money, and employment assignments are administered by a computer system that offers suitable placements on the basis of personal choice and special skills. Places of work are democratically run and no work assignment is compulsory, but a strong moral code and the power of custom makes the task of administration less chaotic than it could be. The persuasive force, and fear, of public opinion also means that people accept work postings in less than ideal circumstances, sometimes to their own detriment. The right to free enterprise on Anarres allows anyone to form their own syndicate and requisition the materials necessary for their project. When Shevek comes up against forces of conservatism he eventually forms a Syndicate of Initiative with his partner Takver and some like-minded friends. The Syndicate sets in train a shockwave on Urras by publishing Shevek's academic work and communicating with physicists on Urras, leading to Shevek boarding a freighter to travel there.

While a part of the novel deals with events on Urras after Shevek's arrival, *The Dispossessed* is also concerned with psychology and the nature of Shevek's personality. Shevek is a loner, a solitary thinker whose meditative character keeps him apart. He dreams often of a wall, a mark of the personal difficulties he often has in relating to other people, and a childhood friend who is alike in this respect suffers grievously because of his own iconoclasm. Shevek comes to understand himself as the anarchist he was brought up to be, and he comes to see that freedom is based on a recognition of human solitude and that this recognition is the only thing that can transcend it. *The Dispossessed* sensitively explores the inescapable dynamic between the existential plight of the individual and the communal pull of the social world, between solitude and solidarity. This dialectic is synthesized in the way that comradeship is seen to be built on a recognition of the pain and loneliness of existence. Shevek remembers witnessing a man die as a result of a work accident – he tends to the victim but, like all of us, the man has to face death by himself, 'I saw that you can't do anything for anyone. We can't save each other. Or ourselves.'[29] This is not a platform for existential despair or mysticism, but a fact of existence that Shevek acknowledges. The predicament of being and the fear of living is a fact to be endured, Beckett-wise, but Shevek builds on it in a search for reconciliation and contentment of a sort. In a conversation between Shevek and a truck driver, where they discuss personal relationships and the eventual ennui that will descend on a life of sex without love, the driver explains his personal Buddhist-like attitude: 'It isn't changing around from place to place that keeps you lively. It's getting time on your side. Working with it, not against it.'[30] The solidarity that comes from shared pain is what allows Shevek to break the ice with Efor, a servant assigned to him by the university on Urras that hosts his trip and who eventually puts him in contact with a political underground on Urras. The existential ideas that move like a current through *The Dispossessed* are related to Le Guin's awareness of the anarchist dimension to Taoism and Buddhism. Life on Anarres, though not through choice on the part of its people, has been harsh and demanding in material ways, but the positive gain is seen to triumph. The desire to possess, to own and to dominate, is replaced with a world that shares material benefits, where work is made as meaningful as possible, power is decentralized and self-realization facilitated, and out of this shedding of desire comes freedom. In the end, *The Dispossessed* is a celebration of anarchism. Shevek is able to challenge certain aspects of life on Anarres because it is an anarchist world. When he leaves on his mission to Urras, a hostile crowd gathers to thwart him and a guard is killed. When Shevek returns to Anarres, the same kind of crowd await him, but there is also a crowd of supporters who have responded to the need to rekindle the revolution.

Cynics are likely to suggest that science fiction is the most suitable form for exploring the unworkable ideals of anarchism, but empirical support for the feasibility of some of the structures of organization that Le

Guin describes is to be found in the history of anarchist-held regions of Spain during the Spanish Civil War. Here, writ large, was a demonstration of the reality of anarchist organization on a widespread and popular scale. What took place and what was established in Spain, described in chapter Five, shared historical space with the very different work of organization unfolding in another part of the continent. In both Spain and Germany issues of class conflict were boiling over, but the kettle was not whistling the same sound. While the Nazi Party was beginning to develop its economic and social programmes, a syndicalist trade union in Spain was putting a different set of principles into practise. The Confederación Nacional del Trabajo (CNT), formed in 1911 and building up to one million members over the next eight years, successfully operated without a paid bureaucracy by using a system of rotating officials who never became permanent. The CNT began with a union at a place of work, which then grouped itself with other unions in the same town and spread out in a regional federation to national level. Majority voting and proportional representation was used to reach decisions, but any decision reached by delegates at national level was subject to ratification by local union members. In terms of organizational strength and ability to operate successfully across a nation state, the CNT could match the Nazi Party by the 1930s. Apart from their totally opposed ideologies, a crucial difference between the CNT and the Nazis was that Hitler would gain the active cooperation of German business interests, and muted tolerance from the governments of their peers in other parts of Europe, while Spanish anarchists would be opposed by reactionary forces, including the Soviet Union. Nevertheless, a large-scale anarchist-inspired organization did exist and function successfully in Spain, and the fact supports the argument that such a form of management and administration is not utopian daydreaming.

Anarchism as a realizable ideal struggles against the ingrained perception that there is something absurdly unworkable about the idea of government without a government, of politics without a centralized, hierarchical state, and organized, purposeful struggle without a Party. Even a historian like Eric Hobsbawm, while acknowledging that 'to be politically conscious in those days [Barcelona in the 1930s] meant to become an anarchist as certainly as in Aberavon it meant to join the Labour Party', nevertheless falls back on the familiar caricature of anarchism as a beautiful but lunatic pipedream, futile by virtue of its purity.[31] It is not felt that there is a need to explain why a political and social consciousness regarded as ludicrous could be an everyday material force in Spanish culture. More churlishly, is it not appropriate to ask – in the light of the history of a Labour Party that abandoned the miners in 1984–5, which was sustained by the faith and idealism of people in places like South Wales – whether the pipe-dream was the belief that a reformist parliamentary party would transform their way of life?

LA BEAUTÉ

EST DANS LA RUE

CHAPTER THREE

Marx, Nietzsche and Anarchism

Saving Marx

The broad span of the anarchist tradition, embracing both anarcho-communism and individualist anarchism, finds metaphysical expression in a philosophical arc framed by Marx on one side and Nietzsche on the other. The degree of overlap between these two thinkers, and the significance attached to the vital differences between them mirrors, in a way, the earlier discussion of the extent to which the claims of communist and individualist anarchism can be reconciled.

An important proviso is that there is a non-negotiable gulf between anarchism and the non-philosophical Marxism that developed in practice after the 1917 Russian Revolution and which was given theoretical justification by Lenin and others. Anarchism is profoundly at odds with the kind of Marxist-Leninism that engendered Marxist parties around the world; parties which are still in existence, even in Western Europe, as if preserved in formaldehyde.[1] The philosophy of Marx, on the other hand, has an enduring importance as a way of understanding the world, and it remains vitally important to anarchist philosophical thought. Not surprisingly, then, the relationship between anarchism and Marx is a stormy and at times a contradictory one, and the personal encounter between Marx and the anarchist Bakunin anticipated the kind of disagreements that would later find expression in the conflicts that scarred the early years of the Russian revolution and the course of the Spanish Civil War in the mid-1930s.

There are many accounts of the personal feud between Marx and Bakunin that culminated at the infamous meeting of the First International at The Hague in 1872.[2] The International Working Men's Association, founded in London in 1864, brought together trade unions and grew every year, until by 1870 it had an estimated membership of 800,000, including Marx and Bakunin. In their clash of opinions neither man comes off in a favourable light, with Bakunin indulging in some atrocious and misguided abuse and Marx stealing the show by manipulating the International's proceedings so as to ensure the defeat of the anarchists. The *coup de grâce* came when two proposals were passed, one to move the headquarters of the International to New York, thereby making it practically impossible for anarchist delegates to attend and thus sidelining their voice, and to expel Bakunin – who didn't attend the meeting – for an alleged fraud and threat of violence. The Hague event is usually portrayed as a clash of personalities, playing up the larger-than-life image of Bakunin, but this masks the doctrinal differences that show Bakunin's criticisms of Marxism to be remarkably prescient and well-founded. Bakunin, opposing any centralization of the International, warned of the danger of authoritarianism and of a red bureaucracy warping the soul of a working-class movement. Marx dismissed such criticism, genuinely fearful that the antics of what he saw as socialist sects could only hold back the movement as a whole, and he failed to see the importance of Bakunin's point.

Bakunin's flamboyant failures at revolutionary politics so alarmed the practical Marx that the latter's mind was clouded by prejudice. Fuelled by an excited imagination that could veer towards fantasy, Bakunin was a professional revolutionary who loved forming secret societies and popping up all over Europe whenever there was the faintest sniff of an insurrection. He interrupted a journey between Paris and Prague once when, passing a group of German peasants making a ruction around a castle, he jumped out of his conveyance and began organizing the rebels and applying his knowledge as an artillery officer in Russia to the task in hand. By the time he got back in the coach, the castle was in flames. He experienced the major revolutions of 1848 and was imprisoned in 1849 for seven years for his activities. Moved from prison to prison until exiled to Siberia, Bakunin managed to escape and ended up in Yokohama where he boarded a ship for San Francisco. Returning to Europe as untamed as ever, he was 56 years of age when in Lyon, before the Paris Commune of 1871, he theatrically seized the town hall and proclaimed from its balcony the abolition of the state.

Bakunin and Marx had once enjoyed one another's politics, a reminder of the fact that they both drank at the wellspring of the French Revolution. Historically, anarchism and Marxism were alike in their common desire to take the revolution of 1789 beyond the demands of the bourgeois class that sought only to replace the old aristocratic social and economic order with their own version. Supporters of Bakunin and Marx shared the same platform space in the First International, until the rupture of 1872 at The Hague. The split led to the word 'anarchist' becoming a term of abuse among Marxists for anyone not prepared to accept the disciplined Party line, while later events under the banner of Soviet Marxism vindicated Bakunin's criticisms. For our examination of anarchism we need to salvage Marx's revolution in philosophy, which is also called Marxism but which shares little else with the centralized Marxist parties that Bakunin correctly predicted would emerge unless a libertarian perspective was adopted.

Social Ontology

Marxism as a philosophy seeks to make sense of the world we live in and to explain why change is possible and desirable. To appreciate the nature of the radical break that Marx made with traditional European philosophy, we might take the philosopher Kant as a representative of the kind of thinking that is being overturned. Kant's account of the nature and limits of our knowledge, his epistemology in other words, remains a cornerstone of accustomed thought about the relationship between us and the way the world is. This is not referring to customary patterns of thought in the field of contemporary academic philosophy, but rather to the way in which Kant's systematic worldview broadly represents the prevailing, conventional way in which many people think about how we come to know about the world. In this sense, Kant's worldview opened a window on the philosophical assumptions that underlay many current patterns of thought.

Any object which is knowable by us, Kant said, must display particular subjective features that are contributed by what he called 'forms of sensibility' and certain *a priori* principles. Space and time are seen as forms of sensibility, and prominent principles are those that regard substance in nature as remaining permanent through change and the idea that every change has a cause. As a result of such forms of sensibilities and *a priori* principles, we have a structure, a form, by which we make sense of an external world, but the fundamental nature of that external world remains beyond our intellectual grasp. Our understanding certainly structures a given, material reality, but the nature of that material reality is ultimately unknowable, and the nature of what Kant calls a 'thing in itself' remains independent of our understanding. It is with this aspect of Kant's philosophy that Marx made a revolutionary and irrevocable break. Marx denies that there is any objective world 'out there' that exists independently of the knowing subject. On first acquaintance, this seems a startling assertion to make. Does he seriously mean that mountains and bicycles have no objective existence, or that genes are like jeans and did not exist until they came to be known? This is indeed what Marx is saying, and the significance of the break with Kantian epistemology that this philosophy represents is as relevant to the philosophy of anarchism as it is to the philosophy of Marxism.

The Kantian view underpins a view of the world that is reinforced on a daily basis by so many forms of representation and so many intellectual disciplines that it seems like pure common sense to say that the world is made up of discrete value-free objects that we, as subjects, observe and contemplate, and about which some of us, as rational scientists, draw logical conclusions and so deduce scientific laws that are then validated through their powers of predictability. New observations, new mathematics or new thoughts – whether Einstein's non-Euclidean world, string theory or whatever – may give rise to new laws of science but all the time the 'really real' fundamental nature of the external world remains, necessarily, beyond our reach. Given that we can never be wholly sure about the fundamental nature of reality, although as subjects we can cleverly exploit what we do observe, we are seemingly locked into, whether we like it or not, a subject–object dualism. This Kantian dualism posits us as the subject and the given world as the object, and Kant himself recognized that the only alternative to his system would be to recognize a dynamic interaction and feedback between subject and object.[3]

For Marx there is no 'thing in itself' because, epistemologically, there is no given world that is simply there, independent of ourselves. Marx is saying that we create the world that we know and it does not exist before we come to know it. This is not idealism – the notion that reality is something confined to the contents of our minds – although, put baldly like this, it certainly seems like a brand of idealism. Marx is not arguing that I as an individual create the world I know. He is arguing instead that there is a dynamic relationship between the subject, the 'I', and the object, the world that seems to exists independently of the 'I'. For Marx, it is this interaction that is fundamental to being. Ontology, the philosophical investigation of existence or being, can only be a social, historical ontology and what is given – that is, Kant's 'thing in itself' – is always our creation and therefore capable of being changed in the most fundamental of ways. History, for Marx, is ontological and not just epistemological. Similarly, ideas are material in the sense that they are inseparable from the lives we lead:

> Morality, religion, metaphysics, all the rest of ideology and their corresponding forms of consciousness, thus no longer retain the semblance of independence . . . men, developing their material production and their material intercourse, alter, along with their real existence, their thinking and the products of their thinking. Life is not determined by consciousness, but consciousness by life.[4]

For Kant there is no possibility of interaction between mind and matter, other than the understanding's *a priori* structuring of reality, and his concern in *The Critique of Pure Reason* is to establish the identity of these structures that are in our minds. For Marx, on the other hand, it is we ourselves, our consciousness and our praxis, that constitutes and changes reality. Just as the physicist cannot work on elementary particles without changing what he studies, so too does the act of knowing change what it contemplates. Marx is not falling into idealist or anti-realist positions for, even though he insists there is no human reality outside of consciousness and intention, it is reality he is talking about and there is, always, a material world that exists. This material world that exists, however, is not a fundamental, ontological given. It is, instead, the result of the dynamic and creative relationship between subject and object.

The importance of Marx's ontology cannot be underestimated because its enduring value contributes hugely to the worth and rigour of anarchism as a philosophy. Anarchism rejects what is here labelled the Kantian worldview, the view that reality is a fixed given, not least because it is just such a point of view that underpins so much of what passes for political philosophy and the social sciences. Reality is accepted as a given and rationalism is equated with a quantitative, 'scientific' approach that collects data, measures and assesses 'facts', tunes and adjusts the system but never questions it in qualitative terms or interrogates its status as part of a 'natural' reality. The singularity of what Marx is saying contributes a vital dimension to anarchism, making the slogan that appeared on the walls of Paris in 1968 – *DEMAND THE IMPOSSIBLE* – less surreal than it sounds. In one sense, the impossible is possible because what seems to be unchangeable is historically contingent and always capable of being changed. Marx describes humanity as an 'objective being', and by this he means that being and consciousness is inseparable from the external objects out of which humanity creates itself and out of which humanity is also conditioned:

> To say that man is a corporeal, living, real, sensuous objective being with natural powers means that he has real, sensuous objects as the object of his being and of his vital expression, or that he can only express his life in real, sensuous objects.[5]

It is through human practice, productive activity, that humanity constitutes its existence; we are who we are because of the way we express our life, and the way we express ourselves is by what we produce and the way we produce it. Physical and mental production changes nature, the world that is both outside of the individual and inside his or her head, and this is what is called history. Hegel contributed the idea of the dialectic as the interaction between subject and object, but Marx, by giving history an ontological identity, makes history (as opposed to consciousness) the very being of reality.

It is Marx's philosophy, his social ontology and the always available potential to change the way things are, that is central to libertarian socialist thought, for anarchism cherishes the realization that the way things are now is not fixed, and what is so often taken for human nature may be the habit of many lifetimes but it is not immutable. Anarchism can be at one with Marx in wanting to bypass philosophical arguments that posit an objective world independent of the subject, preferring to build on a materialist metaphysics that factors in at base level the changeability of the world:

> The question whether objective truth can be attributed to human thinking is not a question of theory, but a practical question. In practice man must prove the truth, that is, the reality and power, the this-sidedness of his thinking. The dispute over the reality or non-reality of thinking which is isolated from practice is a purely scholastic question.[6]

Marx was no utopian and he was not prone to describing or evoking some Edenic life that might be possible in an anarcho-communist future, but he captured with dramatic vividness what life was like under capitalism. He recognized the exciting revolutionary energy of capitalism, how it broke with the past and ushered in a devastating new world order. *The Communist Manifesto* expresses with wondrous admiration the tremendous achievement of capitalism and the way in which it shapes our world.

> The bourgeoisie, wherever it has got the upper hand, has put an end to all feudal, patriarchal, idyllic relations. It has pitilessly torn asunder the motley feudal ties that bound man to his 'natural superiors', and has left remaining no other nexus between man and man than naked self-interest . . . All that is solid melts into air, all that is holy is profaned, and man is at last compelled to face with sober senses, his real conditions of life, and his relations with his kind.[7]

It seems obvious from Marx's critique of the way life is constituted under capitalism, and the way in which its social reality reduces the quality of lived experience, that he is driven by a positive idea of human worth. Such an idea of human worth implies a notion of human nature. Does it not, though, raise a contradiction or at least a paradox? For if all of reality is always brought into being by people and their social practices, and if it is constantly capable of change, how can there be such a thing as human nature? It is in the writings of the young Marx that we find the fullest consideration of this issue, and it is in these writings that anarcho-communism can endorse so much of what Marx is saying. In the *Economic and Philosophical Manuscripts* of 1844, Marx speaks of our essentialist 'species-being' as social animals providing the very bedrock of human existence. It is only in society that the individual manifests his being, for 'man's individual and species-life are not two distinct things'.[8] This is as close as Marx gets to acknowledging some notion of human nature, but it still raises the question of whether he is trying to have his cake and eat it. If our world and our very being is historically specific, how can we fall back on some essentialist idea of what constitutes human existence? The answer may be a paradox, but it is not a contradiction because for Marx, and this comes close to the metaphysical heart of anarchism, there is a Nietzschean dimension to species-being that amounts to a creative, self-realizing urge or process. Life, essentially social as it has to be, has no other purpose than the individual man or woman enjoying the human freedom of creating his or her own being and revelling in its abundant possibilities. It is the very lack of any other purpose to life that gives life its meaning: 'The whole character of a species, its species-character, resides in the nature of its life activity, and free conscious activity constitutes the species-character of man.'[9] What is often understood as human nature is for Marx this life force that exists, he says, within every individual.

For Thomas Hobbes, the seventeenth-century political philosopher, there is no alternative to government other than a life, as he famously put it, that is 'solitary, poor, nasty, brutish, and short'.[10] Government is necessary and desirable, because without it there is no assurance that we will not be at the mercy of others who make their own judgements about what is best. We accept the rule of government in return for a guarantee of our safety and well-being. This seems, at a basic level, to be the way most of us would justify the existence of government as we understand it today. We are willing to go along with it because how else can we have laws and the police to protect us?

Hobbes's views arise from an ontology of the self, which carries with it the notion of an ontological necessity to be selfish. This is not necessarily the same as saying that all human beings are horribly selfish, but it is looking at people as, primarily, individuals. Marx, on the other hand, has an ontology of man as a social being. Our nature, our being, is not a given; we are not born as individuals. Our nature is inseparable from our practices, social and economic and so on, and when our practices change, so too does our sense of our human nature.

Just Great

It is not only Marx's social ontology that illuminates the radical and realizable intent of anarchism to create a new world. The concepts of alienation and commodity fetishism, arising from Marx's analysis of capitalism, feed into the broad anarchist critique of the contemporary world order and, in particular, help explain why stores like Nike, Starbucks and McDonald's have become symbolic targets for the anti-capitalist movement. The Marxist concepts also form part of a response to one of the most familiar arguments trotted out when the terminal decline of socialism is being taken for granted, namely that Marx could not have foreseen the way in which capitalism would adapt and survive by vastly improving the material quality of people's lives and, as a consequence of its success, render archaic the outmoded notion of class conflict.

For Marx, alienation is what happens to people when their work makes them feel separate from themselves and from the wider social community that forms the essential context for meaningful labour. So much employment, whether in the sweatshops of Cambodia or the call centres of Scotland, is a nightmarish inversion of work as an expression of our species-being. Meaningful work, on the other hand, is a communal and human activity because the products of labour not only bear the value of those who make them but they are produced in the conscious knowledge of fulfilling the needs of other people. The mutuality of work is what Marx means when he speaks of man's individual and species-life being not distinct from each other but inter-related. Under capitalism, the opposite is the case because production is geared to profit not need, and most people's work does not allow for the enjoyment of putting themselves into what they produce and of being recognized for this. The experience of employment, for most people, alienates them from themselves and from the products of their work so that what they make become mere objects and this process, says Marx, causes a loss of reality. In the *Economic and Philosophical Manuscripts* of 1844, Marx writes of alienation as a state of non-being – 'What the product of his labour is, he is not'[11] – because of the way work robs people of their species-being and makes what they produce into commodities that have no value for them. An extreme, but logical, example of this was brought alive in a Tel Aviv courtroom in 1961 when Adolf Eichmann spoke calmly and rationally about his work as a Nazi bureaucrat organizing the train journeys that shipped Jews across Europe (arranging the payment of fares to the railways who carried children under the age of 4 for free), and, quite properly as his reason saw it, not concerning himself with the nature of their destination.

While alienation is a familiar term in summaries of Marx's economic analyses, its significance as a human state of being, or rather non-being, is accorded a central role in anarchism's concern with the consequences of the social relations created by capitalism. This is why *Tout va bien* (Just Great), a 1972 film made by Jean-Luc Godard and Jean-Pierre Gorin while supposedly in Maoist mode, is seen to be, surprisingly, nurturing anarchist ideas. The stars of the film, Jane Fonda and Yves Montand, play two left-wing intellectuals, a journalist and commercial film-maker, who find themselves in a food-processing factory when the managing director is detained by striking workers staging a sit-in. The manager delivers an address, pointing out that Marxism never brought the end of alienation in the USSR and claiming that talk of class war is a nineteenth-century idea, out of date in an 'era of evolutionary revolution'. A model of reason, he acknowledges that work can be dull and that materialism isn't everything, but justifies the way things are on the grounds that prosperity and well-being are becoming available for all. The response to the manager's Blairism is enacted by the strikers as they reflect on their alienating work and begin to shrug off passivity without the need of leaders. A trade union official turns up, alarmed at the wildcat action and concerned that matters are getting out of hand, only to be bundled out by the strikers and told to get back to his 'yakety-yak'.

The film's dynamic of reflexivity has Fonda and Montand also responding to what they have seen, questioning their personal relationship and their understanding of politics. They realize that the workers in the factory had been changed by the events of 1968 and were happy to be taking direct action, gleefully insisting that the manager be given only the same short time to urinate as they are allowed, so that eventually he makes his office an improvised *pissoir*. The strikers' spirit of carnivalesque inversion is informed by the anarchist's urge to dismantle hierarchies: 'No more qualifications. No more categories. Seize the time on the assembly line', as one of the women employees announces. Five days later, Fonda and Montand are anxiously sunk in passivity, aware that their activity is only contemplative, and wondering about the future. Unlike them, the workers changed themselves by engaging with and rebelling against the subjectivity of contentment that the manager complacently articulates. As the film draws to an end, there is a scene of Fonda in a vast supermarket 'waiting for new voices' amidst shots of quiescent consumerism that include a left-wing politician selling his party to the shoppers like a special promotion for a discounted washing-powder. This moment is contained within a tracking shot that also catches workers far too engaged in rifling the supermarket shelves to pay attention to his sales spiel. Not surprisingly, *Tout va bien* was criticized by just the kind of politicos and cultural theorists that the film sought to interrogate for their own lack of engagement and soul.

Neo-Marxist sociologists, and many brands of postmodernism, follow in the footsteps of Herbert Marcuse and describe a world of refined and de-alienated subjectivity, where the consumer prisoner plays self-indulgently and contentedly with signs and subject positions. Anarchism has little truck with the theoretical filigree of postmodernism and prefers to acknowledge Marx's alienation as a lived, sensuous reality that is complex but codified, and seeks to replace it with an alternative. Many anarchists want to insist on the sheer shittiness of most work and the way in which life's routines become subordinated to the demands of work. So-called leisure time becomes increasingly occupied by preparing for work, shopping for it, dressing for it, travelling to and from it and, most of all, recuperating from it in order to be able to get through the next day, the next week. However attractive these servicing activities are sculpted to seem, alienation is real, and for many anarchists it fuels the realization that curtailing exploitation must mean changing the way people work. A vision of an egalitarian future is not enough if it ignores the authoritarian forms of organization that structure places of work.

The illusion of a consumer-driven but happy world is facilitated by a whole gamut of professions and discourses that, one way and another, posit a Kantian world of objects and people existing in value-free, objective isolation. The primary example of this is labour, understood as possessing a quantitative exchange value as opposed to a qualitative use value. The same logic invites an obsession with having and possessing, an alienation of our being which is made easy when value is bracketed off by making everything ownable, usable and quantifiable. Thus, economists can calculate a happy marriage as worth £70,000 a year and a state of good health some £200,000, and *Harry Potter* novels can be packaged as the literary equivalent of fast food.[12] Such public examples are parts of a process that also changes consciousness, and a prescient description of an aspect of modern consciousness provided by Marx:

> The less you eat, drink, buy books, go to the theatre, go dancing, go drinking, think, love, theorize, sing, paint, fence etc., the more you save and the greater will become the treasure which neither moths nor maggots can consume – your capital. The less you are, the less you give expression to your life, the more you have, the greater your alienated life . . . everything which you are unable to do, your money can do for you.[13]

By the time of *Capital*, Marx has another term, the fetishism of commodities, to describe the way in which commodities take on a mystical, quasi-religious power over those who produce them. But, in the privatization of the self, what reification fails to account for – that which is not reducible to the market and does not possesses merely a monetary value – doesn't go away, just as people don't stop having arms when their height is being measured. What does happen is that attitudes and feelings not conducive to the market-place, and which cannot easily be subsumed into the general commodification of life, are relegated to the private sphere. Hence the world that is so familiar to us, one in which people can be selfless towards their family and friends but not to work colleagues or strangers. In our daily lives we are aware of the need to make this distinction, just as we are aware of the way money devalues what is really precious. So among family and friends the giving of a present is recognized as an act that is qualitatively unlike any exchange in the market-place, which helps explain the unease in using a gift token as a present. Using a gift token, seen as a poor excuse for a cash payment, brings home the recognition that money bypasses the value that can still adhere to material, non-reified objects. Marx brings a sense of value back into philosophy, as opposed to the Kantian-like 'objectivity' of science that separates questions of value from questions of factual knowledge.

By way of a postscript to Marxist philosophy, it is notable that the story of Russia's evolution from the heady vortex of revolutionary Bolshevism to the rigid statism of the USSR is accompanied by an equally dispiriting abandonment of Marx's radical ontology in favour of a vulgar materialism and realism. Under Lenin and his followers there was a return to what was basically a Kantian epistemology that resurrected a narrow concern with subject–object dualism. This retrograde step was expressed in terms of a non-dialectical concept of absolute (Marxist-Leninist) knowledge and absolute truth, something that naturally facilitated the ideological dictatorship that manifested itself in USSR-style Marxism.[14]

What remains is the continuing relevance to anarchism of Marx's ontology, a relevance that withstands the categorical gulf between the practices of Marxism and anarchism. Even though the nature of this gulf was revealing itself as early as the days of Bakunin's clash with Marx, it was never a clash addressing issues relating to Marx's ontology, supporting the idea that the unbridgeable differences between the two practices are not to be located in the strictly philosophical content of Marx's thought. While there is a lot more to Marxism than just the aspects of his philosophy outlined here, including the whole question of the extent to which Marx's own broadly philosophical views changed from those expressed in his early writings, this does not diminish the ongoing importance of Marx's ontology, his ideas of alienation and commodity fetishism, and the class exploitation at the heart of capitalism, to the anarchist perspective.

The social anarchism of anarcho-communism, advocating a communally directed libertarian society, has its metaphysical underpinning in Marx's philosophy.

Marxism has an long-overdue appointment with anarchism, one that Marx himself was reluctant to make and one that Lenin erased for some 70 years. Now, finally freed from the shackles of Soviet statism, the time has arrived for that appointment to be met.

Nietzschean Anarchism

Nietzsche, some of whose ideas overlap with those of Marx, gives abundant philosophical expression to the individualist strand of anarchism. But just as Marx's philosophy has to be disinterred from the kind of Marxism we have grown to know and often loathe, an appreciation of Nietzsche's ideas in relation to anarchism has to be disentangled from a web of misunderstanding and confusion that so easily arises from the difficulty of reading him.

Nietzsche writes of historical man (to use his own term) projecting his basic drives on reality, a process of reordering that involves the repression of some instincts alongside the creative nourishing of others. History is a dynamic and dialectical process of externalizing the self, and it possesses a liberating aspect: 'And life itself confided this secret to me: "Behold," it said, "I am that which *must overcome itself again and again*".' [15] This self-realizing urge, Nietzsche's commonly misunderstood will to power, is not an abstract force but something that takes shape within an historically specific context. In this way, both Marx and Nietzsche regard humanity as beings rooted in contingent, historical circumstances and striving to expand their powers. Anarchists warmly embrace both ideas.

As important as this similarity between Marx and Nietzsche is, an important qualification remains. Marx's view of life as an essentially social process but one where, ideally, people enjoy the human freedom of creating their own being, cannot be conflated with Nietzsche's will to power. The life force, the self-realizing being of becoming, in Marx's ontology is not the same as the will to power. Far from it, given that Nietzsche's notion of the self as a plurality of energy driven drives has a radical, anti-realist edge. What is also lacking in Nietzsche is the Marxist concern with the social, productive activity of humanity. Instead, Nietzsche speaks of man as an 'endangered animal'[16] that seeks protection through cooperation and becomes conscious only after a violent and painful sundering from its animal existence. Looking at society in this way, Nietzsche's accounts – for there is never just one account – of world history can be read as inhumanely nihilistic and of little concern to anarchists. However, always embedded within one reading of Nietzsche are contrary layers of meaning and significance. He also writes of how the human species, once in society, 'arouses interest, tension, hope, almost certainty for himself, as though something were being announced through him, were being prepared, as though man were not an end but just a path, an episode, a bridge, a great promise . . .'.[17] This Promethean strain can be found in both thinkers, with Marx speaking of the birth of a proletariat that will change history and Nietzsche speaking of man's sickness in modern society as being an illness, but an illness, as he puts it, like pregnancy. The striking similarities between the two thinkers are not just expressed at the level of metaphor. They both criticize modern society as dysfunctional because of the way it thwarts human activity. For Marx the criticism is directed at the social consequences of an economic order that alienates the majority of those producing goods over which they exercise no control. The result is a reified consciousness, an ideology that allows the workings of market forces to appear natural and eternal, and a commodity fetishism that ultimately makes people unhappy. For Nietzsche, on the other hand, the criticism is directed at the psychological consequences of a social order that insists on simplistically transforming merely human concepts into eternal truths.

Where one speaks of ideologies and alienation, the other refers to idols and psychological sickness.

Nietzsche argues that humans have always needed a set of beliefs, or horizons, to calm the meaningless and chaotic currents of life and make existence bearable; the belief in God being a prime example of what he calls ascetic, life-denying, ideals.[18] The Enlightenment has seen off this belief – Nietzsche's famous death of God – but left humans in a nihilistic state because they have found nothing with which to replace God. In a parallel movement to Marx's claim that bourgeois relationships are smuggled into our consciousness as natural laws, Nietzsche castigates the way in which a herd morality passes itself off as Truth. God is dead but the poisonous belief in sin and guilt has not vanished so easily because humans still want their illusions.[19] Behind the illusion of a now-defunct Christianity there still functions – and this is part of the modern sickness that Nietzsche rails against – the atheistic illusion of the self as an ego, as a subject, when there should be just a sane and healthy commitment to aimless becoming and emergence. While many anarchists would not be as extreme as Nietzsche in this respect, they would endorse his assault on herd morality and the fear of living that can eat into and sap one's capacity to live life to the full.

Where all but the most individualist anarchist would part company with Nietzsche is around the point where his ontology begins to shear away from Marx's. Although both thinkers are materialists, Nietzsche sees science (though not his own 'gay science') and rationality as part of the sickness because of the way they reify and fetishize the world as things about which facts can be discovered.[20] His critique is far more radical than Marx because he is not just attacking empiricism and positivism but the very idea, even when expressed in Marx's anti-Kantian and dialectical sense, of the human being as a subject that relates to objects. For Nietzsche, the subject is not a subject but a creative becoming, a fusion of drives fuelled by will.[21] The difference between the two thinkers begins to seem unbridgeable: Marx seeks the truth behind false consciousness and ideologies whereas Nietzsche regards truth itself as an idol and an illusion to which the modern world is still enslaved. Marx sees humanity expressing itself in work, a wide-ranging activity capable of overcoming the narrow, alienated experience it has become for so many people, whereas Nietzsche stresses purposeless play and prodigality as expressing the will to power. The more unbridgeable appears the gulf between Marx and Nietzsche, the more unbridgeable seems the gulf between communist anarchists and individualist anarchists.

Notwithstanding the deep differences between the two thinkers, it remains open whether Nietzsche is irrevocably at odds with Marx; for just as conversation between communist anarchism and individualist anarchism is viable, so too is a synthesis, however selective its basis, of Marx and Nietzsche. Both thinkers contribute to anarchism by showing why people would be happier without capitalism, and Nietzsche is as cogent as anti-capitalist protestors in questioning the rampant logic of the market-place: 'The man engaged in commerce understands how to appraise everything without having made it . . . "Who and how many will consume this?" is his question of questions.'[22] Nietzsche castigates the consequences of a work ethic that makes one so ashamed of resting that prolonged relaxation induces an anxiety, a fear of forgetting a cardinal principle of capitalist metaphysics – 'Rather do anything than nothing.'[23] Nietzsche assaults the spiritual enfeeblement of a consumer society, but, instead of viewing it as the product of a class-based power system, he fixes on the psychological damage caused by a slavish entrapment to money that becomes an end in itself rather than a means to the play of desire.

As welcome as Nietzsche's attacks on the work ethic are, it should not imply a blindness to those aspects of Nietzsche's thought that are frankly antagonistic to all but the most extreme and selfish forms of individualist anarchism. Nietzsche may well have known Max Stirner's work, for there are echoes of it in his own writings, and there is a key difference between

Marx's ideal of purposive self-realization through labour in an anarcho-communist community and Nietzsche's acceptance of exploitation and a limited notion of private property as essential aspects of the will to power. The repressive nature of work, which for Marx is the consequence of an historically specific mode of production, is a psychic given in Nietzsche's mental landscape.

The tension between Nietzsche and Marx reflects the lines of stress within anarchism between notions of complete personal, individual autonomy and those of communistic, social freedom. Marx's anarcho-communist society is a social endeavour, based on sharing, but Nietzsche's overman is an autonomous being necessarily at odds with any communal ethos. The overman is a value-creating creature who wilfully and necessarily defies the herd mentality of lesser mortals and affirms truth-making as an individual's interpretative activity. Despite the fact that Marx and Nietzsche both contribute something valuable to anarchism, they are probably within their own terms finally incompatible. Marx could call Nietzsche bourgeois for failing to analyze the historical determinants of his own beliefs and, in riposte, Marx could be accused by Nietzsche of bourgeois thinking for believing in idols like truth and reason. Socialism and anarchism for Nietzsche were just more metaphysical illusions, pernicious ones because of their espousal of communal endeavour at the expense of the free individual.

Anarchism, of course, is not beholden to the entirety of any system of thought, so the challenge of trying to synthesize Marx and Nietzsche is only critical in so far as it mirrors difficulties in reconciling communist anarchism with the more extreme versions of its individualist wing. Push individualism far enough and it intrudes into the gun-toting, right-wing libertarianism domiciled in the US, or the Thatcherite notion that there is no such thing as society. To conclude on such a sour note would be an injustice to Nietzsche, burdening him with a legacy he no more deserves than the accusations of anti-semitism and a proto-Nazism. It is Marx who carries unwholesome baggage, of the authoritarian sort that Bakunin recognized so long ago, but both Nietzsche and Marx, in their own ways, contribute a great deal to the integrity of anarchism. Marx's ontology and his analysis of capitalism as a revolutionary, world-changing fundamentalism is central to communist anarchism, and other aspects of Marxist thought, especially alienation and commodity fetishism, are gladly taken on board. Neither anarchists nor Marx imagine that communism equals utopia. Marx believed that only after the advent of a communist society would human history begin, a history wherein humans direct their society, and anarchists are at one with this.

In a similar spirit of judicious assimilation, Nietzsche's subversive attack on the psychology of conformity, his life-affirming championing of the self's creative becoming, and the assault on notions of truth and reason at the expense of history and being are all warmly embraced in the spirit of individualism that infuses anarchism. And just as anarchism has no truck with Marxist and Marxist-Leninist ideas of the party and the state, so too does it distance itself from aspects of Nietzsche that are incompatible with libertarian socialism. The will to power as a ceaseless process of exploitation and domination is rejected in favour of readings of Nietzsche that point to more progressive implications of his ideas. Radical ecology and the environmentalist wing of the anti-capitalist movement can find philosophical support in a green reading of Nietzsche, one that emerges from an admittedly selective interpretation of some of his central ideas. Nietzsche's insistence that humans are driven by a will to power, subject to misinterpretation as a proto-fascistic ideology, is rooted in the primacy that Nietzsche gives to the instincts and to his view of humans as beings that share very fundamental characteristics with other animals. As a naturalist, Nietzsche entirely rejects notions of any metaphysical essence to humanity and prioritizes instead a material substratum of suffering, death, non-purposive appearance and ceaseless flux. Reason is not a criterion of reality but rather a way, a means, of mastering and ordering reality, and by this means humans posit their own little worlds. These worlds, created and sustained by our energy, are not intrinsically superior to the worlds of other creatures that inhabit a common earth. Nietzsche attacks what he calls atomism as an exemplar of the Kantian worldview that supports much of modern scientific thinking. Regarding atoms as providing a structure for an ultimate realm of existence is a form of epistemological solitariness, as if things existed in isolation from other things instead of being related to everything else. Science functions as a utilitarian and simplistic ordering of reality that justifies a sense of mastery, whereas Nietzsche seeks to de-prioritize the supremacy given to the human world in favour of a radical equality that puts humans and animals on the same stage of existence. It is possible to read Nietzsche's world – a ceaseless and aimless recycling of becoming and unbecoming – in ecological terms as a complex, organic whole. In these terms, Nietzsche's account supports the idea of the earth as a holistic but finite given of which we are but one part, and as a finite whole it cannot be raided in a destructive and exploitative manner.[24]

Many anarchists are not alarmed at the dialectic of anarchism, the tension between communalism and individualism, and prefer to seize on it as the dynamic that will drive anarchism forward into uncharted areas. Socialism without its soul in the individual is as hollow as individual freedom without a communist commitment. What Nietzsche calls the will to power is softened by an anarchist interpretation that champions an individual's life as an experiential force that seeks self-expression as naturally as a plant grows towards the light, and which strives to progress as part of a social whole. This insistence on the value of freedom distinguishes anarchism from traditional communism because freedom must structure the organizations formed to bring about social change, as Bakunin explained:

> Equality without freedom is the despotism of the state . . . the most fatal combination that could possibly be formed, would be

to unite socialism to absolutism; to unite the aspiration of the people for material well-being . . . with the dictatorship or the concentration of all political and social power in the state . . . We must seek full economic and social justice only by way of freedom. There can be nothing living or human outside of liberty, and a socialism that does not accept freedom as its own creative principle . . . will inevitably . . . lead to slavery and barbarism.[25]

CHAPTER FOUR

Attacking the State

Direct Action

Anarchists attack the state in myriad acts of rebellion and disobedience and in countless different ways – symbolically, conspiratorially, publicly, violently, peacefully, surreptitiously, artistically, criminally, legally – always sharing a wish for direct action of one kind or the other. Sometimes, as with the propaganda of the deed at the end of the nineteenth century, the subject of the action is an individual regarded as a representative of the state; sometimes, as with the Angry Brigade in Britain in the 1970s, the physical fabric of an institution or organization is attacked because of what it represents. As will be seen, there have been times when promoting anarchism becomes an all-out military necessity, as during the Spanish Civil War in 1936. The different circumstances of our age see the anti-capitalist movement using mass action, but without relying on physical violence, to confront intra-state institutions. Different levels of consciousness among those attacking the state allow for a broad understanding of what constitutes anarchist direct action, blurring the distinction that many people make between 'riot and revolt, between crime and revolution'.[1] Such a distinction is not always as pertinent to anarchists as it is to professional historians, but this chapter, none the less,

81

restricts itself to attacks on the state that are self-consciously anarchist in inspiration or at least recognizably anarchist in their sensibility.

The world's earliest known example of politically aware anarchism in action can be traced in the events of April 1649, when Gerrard Winstanley and some 40 settlers established an agrarian, proto-anarchist community on common and waste land at St George's Hill, Surrey (now an exclusive private housing estate). They were the Diggers, the most radical of the left-wing groups that emerged around the time of the English Civil Wars of the mid-seventeenth century, and their stated intention was to 'work in right-eousness and lay the foundations of making the earth a common treasure for all'.[2] Kevin Brownlow and Andrew Mollo's 1975 film *Winstanley* meticu-lously recreates the historical record of what took place at St George's Hill and, while not seeking to consciously promote the anarchist impulse behind the movement, the film makes clear the engagement made with libertarian communism in Winstanley's pamphlets and in the direct action of the Diggers.

Winstanley, after failing to succeed his father as a textiles merchant, became a labourer and radical thinker, and his writings reveal the subver-sive intent of the Diggers at St George's Hill. Landless squatters they may have been, but as they cleared and manured the common land and planted vegetables they were consciously setting out to establish the viability of an alternative way of living, and in the same year Winstanley expressed his awareness of the challenge they were enacting. Freedom, he wrote, 'is the man that will turn the world upside down, therefore no wonder he hath enemies'.[3] In the *True Levellers' Standard* he argued that people's inherent ability to reason and structure their lives removes the perceived necessity for external control and need not therefore 'run abroad after any teacher and ruler without him'. The submission to imposed authority is detrimental as well as unnecessary, for it is the 'ruling and teaching power without [that] doth dam up the spirit of peace and liberty, first within the heart, by filling it with slavish fears of others, secondly without, by giving the bodies of one to be imprisoned, punished and oppressed by the outward power of another'.[4] The community at St George's Hill was established to show how people could live without the need of a governing state and its coercive powers, and by doing so attract more supporters, who would swell its numbers and influence. What was being rejected along with the state and its apparatus was the corrupting notion of private property:

> Let all men say what they will, so long as such are Rulers as call the Land theirs, upholding this particular propriety of *Mine* and *Thine*, the common people shall never have their liberty, nor the Land ever [be] freed from troubles, oppressions and complainings.[5]

Brownlow and Mollo's film also introduces the Ranters, an obscure sect of lifestyle anarchists, whose sexual libertarianism and blasphemous dissent prefigures a cultural battleground that would reappear centuries later. Peter Marshall's study concludes that while an uncertainty surrounds the nature and influence of the Ranters, there is little doubting their status as individualist anarchists.[6] An antinomian faction, their radicalism was expressed in the language of religion, combining the Quaker principle that spiritual well-being had no need for clergy or dogma with a residue of the spirit of the medieval millenarian groups that rejected Church morality and looked to a Second Coming when Christ would establish a state of utopian bliss for 1,000 years before the final Judgment. Like the millenarians, the Ranters saw property and sex as communal gifts of nature, and no laws or moral constraints were binding on the free spirit. *Winstanley* highlights the tension generated between the Ranters and the Diggers in a way that anticipates the touchy sectarianism that can sometimes have macho 'class warrior'-style anarchists dismissing libertarians like Emma Goldman. The championing of sexual and social liberation that Goldman espoused is sometimes seen as limiting to hardcore anarchists, who see it as a distraction from the serious unfinished business of class war. Yet the Diggers and the Ranters were alike in their seditious rejection of the state, and the writings of the Ranter Abiezer Coppe – 'give, give, give, give up your houses, horses, goods, gold, Lands, give up, account nothing your own, have ALL THINGS common'[7] were deemed sufficiently subversive to warrant an Act of Parliament outlawing them.

For the local landowners around St George's Hill, the differences between Diggers and Ranters were less important than their alarming similarities. With the aid of the magistrates and the clergy they set out to destroy what they stood for, and the Diggers' settlement withstood harassment until it was finally suppressed after a year by state power. Phoenix-like, 200 years later, like-minded endeavours reappeared in England during the 1890s. One of the more enduring was the Whiteway Colony near Stroud in Gloucestershire, which began with the purchase of 40 acres of land and the subsequent symbolic burning of the land deeds to inaugurate the communitarian principles of the community.[8] The Whiteway Colony was inspired by Tolstoy, who along with Kropotkin (who provided the stimulus for two other settlements in the north of England in the 1890s) and Bakunin make up that remarkable, aristocratic trinity of nineteenth-century Russian anarchists. Kropotkin was born in 1842 into a landowning family that owned an estate with 12,000 serfs, but five years of travel in Siberia and a trip to western Europe, where he made contact with the First International, resulted in his conversion to anarchism. After terms of imprisonment in Russia and France, he eventually settled in London in his mid-forties and lived there for over 40 years, returning to Russia, after the 1917 Revolution, where he spent the last three years of his life and where over 100,000 attended his funeral.

These nineteenth-century anarchists, like Marx himself, have their visionary politics rooted in the epochal events of the French Revolution

and, for the history of anarchism, it is difficult to overestimate the importance of what took place in Paris. The storming of the Bastille, led by
Théroigne de Méricourt dressed as an Amazon, was direct action of a new
kind, and even though the Revolution descended into the Terror and the
dictatorship of Napoleon, and despite the fact that it laid the foundations
for a new middle-class political order in the form of a centralized state, it
unleashed the force of popular mass discontent. The power of such a
force and the fear it holds for ruling classes has reverberated for over two
centuries, continuing to shape the course of history, and it is not a coincidence that the French Revolution saw the beginning of the challenge to
the negative use of the term anarchist. In September 1793, a group
addressed the Convention:

> We are poor and virtuous *sans-culottes* . . . we know whom our
> friends are: those who have delivered us from the clergy and
> nobility, from the feudal system . . . those whom the aristocrats
> have called anarchists.[9]

Different orders of discourse attach themselves to the French Revolution,
and from an anarchist perspective what was achieved is not invalidated
by the fact that the upheaval replaced the feudal rule of an aristocracy by
an emergent capitalism. What was revealed in the process was another
fact, the realization that an entrenched, seemingly natural, political and
social order could be overthrown. This dimension to the action remains
part of its material history. In 1793, especially, there was a communitarian spirit of revolt that could be heard in a chance remark by one woman
to another on the street – 'You have a pretty dress. Be patient; before
long, if you have two, you will give me one and that's how we want it to
be; it will be like that with everything else'[10] – and heard in the call to
direct action of one of the *Enragés*, Jacques-Roux, that anticipated the
sentiment of the Class War group in Britain some 200 years later,

applauding looting as a means of redistributing wealth. Jacques-Roux's protestation that 'Freedom is but an empty phantom if one class of men can starve another with impunity'[11] was based on the sound anarcho-communist principle that political revolt without social revolution is as hollow as the knowledge that the doors of the Ritz are freely open to anyone who can pay the bill.

The events of the French Revolution also canonized the belief for many would-be insurrectionists that direct action of a mass nature could be provoked into existence by subversive plotting of a conspiratorial nature. Bakunin remains the exemplar of this doomed approach, but his activities criss-crossing Europe and fermenting among others ideas of libertarian revolt, and those of a more philosophical persuasion like Kropotkin a generation later, were vital in spreading anarchist ideas, and it was not only in Europe that their books and essays were translated and widely circulated. The Italian anarchist Errico Malatesta travelled to the USA and Argentina in the 1880s, propagating alternatives to Marxist-inspired vanguard parties; and a decade later an intense young man named Alexander Berkman went to Pittsburgh from New York deter-mined to transplant propaganda by the deed from Europe to the New World. Berkman, born in Lithuania in 1870, emigrated to New York at the age of eighteen and met Emma Goldman, another Russian immigrant, who was working in a clothing factory.

Berkman was in his early twenties when he and Goldman planned a dramatic strike against capitalism, the assassination of Henry Clay Frick, the businessman in charge of a Carnegie steel works who had hired 300 strike-breakers from the Pinkerton Detective Agency men to crush union resistance during an industrial dispute, resulting in the death of ten men. Despite being shot three times and stabbed twice by Berkman in 1892, Frick survived and Berkman was sentenced to 22 years behind bars. His *Prison Memoirs of an Anarchist* (1912), a minor classic of prison literature, bears eloquent and painful testimony to Berkman's youthful idealism, unbearably long periods of solitary confinement, protests against inhuman conditions, despair and loneliness and fruitless escape plans. Released in 1906 and reunited with Goldman, Berkman returned to anarchist agitation, dying in 1936 when he chose suicide rather than continue suffering pain from a prostrate condition and dependency on the financial support of friends. Had he lived just a little longer, some solace at least would have come from hearing about the tumultuous events that were erupting in Spain.

Over the course of his fourteen years imprisonment, Berkman deepened his understanding of the world: 'But maturity has clarified the way', he confided in a letter to Goldman after ten years inside, and experience taught him the need for 'the purified vision of hearts that grow not cold'.[12] Such a remark sounds dryly intellectual, but Berkman's memoirs are rooted in the sensual deprivation of prison, and he grew in intelligence as the years passed, so that the man who walks free at the book's end bravely but fearfully embraces his freedom. In time, Berkman came to see the limitations of violence as a response to the inequities of capitalism.

Both Berkman and Goldman were expelled from the USA for their anti-war activities during World War I and they went to Russia, warmed by the revolutionary fires burning there. Anarchism had been alive and well in pre-revolutionary Russia and anarchists were in the thick of the struggle that followed the first revolution that erupted in February 1917, but when it came to decisive action they were wrong-footed and outclassed by the more disciplined party machinery of the Bolsheviks.

The fortified island city of Kronstadt, 30 kilometres west of St Petersburg and with a population of some 50,000 inhabitants, was not only a vital naval base, it was a centre for anarchist communists. Almost immediately after the October revolution of 1917, Kronstadt found itself on a collision course with Lenin's autocratic government, and by 1921 matters had come to a head. The rationale for Lenin's decision to crush dissent at Kronstadt, used at the time and repeated by Marxist-Leninist parties ever since, was that Bolshevism was in a perilous state and under constant threat from anti-revolutionary forces seeking to restore capitalism. The records show that Kronstadt, far from being a base for such reactionary forces, was calling instead for the aims of the revolution to be pushed forward. The statements and reports issued in the *Izvestia* of the Provisional Revolutionary Committee of Kronstadt make this clear, calling for a 'third, genuinely proletarian revolution', attacking the absolutism and dictatorial intent of 'the old firm of Lenin, Trotsky and Co.' and expressing alarm at the creation of a system of state capitalism that would not change the alienation of working life.[13] Trotsky gave his famous order to the Red Army to shoot the Kronstadters like rabbits; the men's families were taken as hostages and as many as 18,000 were killed when the island was attacked across the frozen ice.[14] By the end of the year, not surprisingly, Goldman and Berkman had had enough and they left Russia.

Kronstadt, far from being an isolated incident, was only the most dramatic and best-remembered episode in the history of anarchist opposition to the Bolshevik state. The honeymoon that had seen anarchists and Bolsheviks on the same side of the barricades only lasted a few months after the revolution of October 1917, and the events at Kronstadt were paralleled further to the south in the Ukraine between 1918 and 1921. There, in an area with a population of some seven million people, anarchists groups established their own communist society. The inspirational individual associated with the movement, Nestor Makhno, was personally courted by Lenin for as long as he could help defend the country against Western armies and reactionary forces threatening the Revolution. For more than a year, the Ukraine remained beyond Bolshevik control and Makhno's forces moved through the countryside in the same spirit as Spanish anarchist militias would do less than twenty years later in Aragón. Echoing the kind of event dramatized in Ken Loach's film about the Spanish Civil War, *Land and Freedom* (1995), revolutionary partisans would move into a district and place collectivization on the agenda but not impose their views, as their public notices made clear:

> This [Makhnovist] army does not serve any political party, any power, any dictatorship . . . It is up to the workers and peasants to act, to organise themselves, to reach mutual understanding in all fields of their lives . . . [The Makhnovists] cannot, and, in any case, will not govern them or prescribe for them in any way.[15]

Makhno himself developed into a paradoxical character, and his alcoholism affected his behaviour in ways that did little credit to himself or to the movement. Not always a model anarchist, he and some of his associates adopted at times a coercive attitude towards 'free' love. They were mostly uneducated peasants and Makhno himself was prone to a reckless heedlessness, but there is no doubting their principled opposition to Bolshevik state capitalism and, unlike Lenin, Trotsky and Co., they were not intent on imposing a one-dimensional state on the Ukraine. As with Kronstadt, the Bolshevik government had no intention of allowing a free-wheeling Makhnovism to challenge its authority, and it demanded submission. Resistance was met with armed suppression and executions, though Makhno managed to escape and finally settled in Paris, where he died a broken and dispirited man in 1935.

The Bolshevik state responded to the Makhnovist movement no differently from any capitalist state threatened with a force that questioned its legitimacy. Anarchism was suppressed from April 1918 onwards, and by 1921 the movement was on its knees. In the summer of that year, Lenin's government imprisoned in Odessa the members of a fairly large and important anarchist group, some of whom were later executed, for spreading propaganda in Soviet institutions and circles, including the Odessa Soviet and the Bolshevik Party's local committee. This, the Party press stated, constituted a treasonous offence, and, from the state's point of view, considering the task it faced both nationally and internationally at the time, it is not difficult to see why they found such a charge an appropriate one. For the same reason, nearly 100 Tolstoyan pacifist anarchists were executed, most for refusing to serve in the Red Army.[16] Anarchists today refer to the events that took place in Russia between 1917 and 1921, not boorishly to show how perfidious the Bolsheviks were, but to illustrate how even left-wing revolutionary states will behave in ways not dissimilar from those of capitalist governments. What happened in Russia under Lenin, long before Stalin arrived on the scene, would be repeated on a smaller scale by a Communist government in Cuba in the 1960s.[17] In between events in Russia and Cuba, it was Spain that disillusioned a generation of communists for whom the earlier events in Russia had not been sufficiently well known, causing them to abandon the hope that all socialists, united as they were by a hatred of capitalism, could find common ground in the task of deconstructing capitalism and building a new and better society.

Meriting Kisses

It was in Spain, during the years of the 1936–9 civil war, that the anarchist tradition had the most striking and at times dramatically successful and inspiring consequences. The Spanish libertarian tradition goes back to the late nineteenth century, to the days when farmers armed with scythes marched into Jerez in 1892 proclaiming that 'we cannot wait another day – we must be the first to begin the revolution – long live Anarchy!'[18] Such moments signalled a strand of militant anarchism in Spain that by the 1930s had led to the development of the 10,000- to 30,000-strong Federación Anarquista Ibérica (FAI), a federation that influenced the country's syndicalist trade union, the CNT.

Syndicalism, a militant form of trade unionism that had mushroomed in western Europe in the early decades of the twentieth century, was scuppered by the catastrophic events of World War I and failed to regain its influence – except in Spain. Here, the libertarian principles of syndicalism, principally its autonomy from political parties, its decentralized, federal, anti-bureaucratic structure, and its long-term aim of undermining capitalism through direct action, attracted revolutionary anarchists from the FAI. By the early 1930s, the CNT was largely dominated by anarchists and had become an anarcho-syndicalist, mass trade-union movement. It was especially influential in the region of Spain stretching from Catalonia to Andalusia, embracing at least half of all trade unionists in the country, though colliding with the socialist Unión General de Trabajadores (UGT). Although committed to non-voting in elections, many CNT members questioned their allegiance to this policy after the election of a national, right-wing government in 1933 and seem to have received some unofficial support from the union when many of them cast their votes in the 1936 general election that brought victory to a Popular Front coalition of left-wing parties.

The Spanish Civil War broke out in July 1936 when the Fascist-inspired General Franco turned on the newly elected government, with the bulk of the army supporting him. Urban workers and peasants responded to the attempted coup with nothing less than a social revolution. In Barcelona prisons were opened, and brothels closed down in accordance with a sentiment expressed shortly earlier in an anarchist publication: 'He who buys a kiss puts himself on the level of the woman who sells it. Hence an anarchist must not purchase kisses. He should merit them.'[19] Mobilizing themselves for defence, militias were formed, land and factories and other work places were collectivized, and the profit motive was consigned to the dustbin of history. Covering an area of over 15 million acres and affecting some three million people, around 2000 collectives were organized that broadly followed anarchist principles. The collectives varied in size and distribution, concentrated mostly in Aragón,

Catalonia and the Levante, as well as in and around Madrid, and were mostly, though not always, organized voluntarily. Large private estates were expropriated, although there were many instances of individual smallholders choosing to remain outside the collectives.

The anarcho-syndicalist CNT and the anarchist FAI both had moderate and extreme wings, and tensions naturally developed within each of them, as well as between them, but neither became a vanguard party intent on imposing, or even introducing, Leninist-style methods of economic organization. As their militias moved across the countryside and into towns and villages, the plan was to persuade the local population to take over the land and factories and run them for themselves along anarcho-communist lines. Local authority was exercised by committees, and the details of their methods and systems of distribution varied from one area to another. Anarchist- and communist-inspired principles led to the pooling of basic food necessities that were then distributed either on a rationing basis or, more commonly, by devising a system of allowances for each family according to the size of the household. Everyday services like medical care were freely provided, and collectives requiring specific resources such as certain raw materials or equipment made requests through the local committee.

Ambitious programmes of self-management got underway in the towns and cities, often with remarkable success, and nowhere more so than in Barcelona. There, the managers of the private General Tramway Company, employing some 7,000 workers, most of whom were members of the CNT, deserted their posts in the revolutionary turmoil and the workers took over their tasks with enthusiasm. A union-appointed commission met with delegates from related work places like the electric power station, repair yards and the administration offices and in less than a week after the street fighting had finished there were 700 tramcars trundling across the city. Painted diagonally across their sides in red and black, this was a hundred more than the usual number of trams that serviced the city due to a decision by the workers to do away with the accident-prone trailer-carriages. The entire tramway system was organized and run on a federalist management basis, coordinating with engineers to make other improvements, for example the replacement of electricity bearing poles with a system of aerial suspension. Even after paying for new tools and equipment purchased from abroad, increasing wages and improving employees' amenities, and introducing a new flat fare system, an operating surplus accrued due to the absence of profit-making and the high salaries paid previously for company executives. There are many examples suggesting that the revolution had a positive effect on economic performance and motivation, and the available evidence also suggests that agricultural production increased between 1936 and 1937.[20] At the same time, though, this period was a war crisis, and statistics cannot simply be taken as a model for what might happen in peacetime. The war affected many aspects of the economic organization of life, and the challenging task of arranging the distribution of goods and services on a national rather than a merely local level was hardly allowed the opportunity of implementation. Nevertheless, the evidence as a whole suggests a remarkable ability on the part of collectives to administer their own affairs on a non-profit basis and run farms and thousands of businesses along participatory lines without state or party control. In Barcelona, the Catalonian capital, everything from shoe-shining to sanitation was brought under public control, as George Orwell witnessed:

> Every shop and café had an inscription saying that it has been collectivised; even the bootblacks had been collectivised and their boxes painted red and black. Waiters and shop-workers looked you in the face and treated you as an equal. Servile and even ceremonial forms of speech had temporarily disappeared . . . There were no private motor cars, they had all been

commandeered, and all the trams and taxis and much of the other transport were painted red and black . . . Above all, there was a belief in the revolution and the future, a feeling of having suddenly emerged into an era of equality and freedom . . . In the barbers' shops were Anarchist notices (the barbers were mostly Anarchists) solemnly explaining that barbers were no longer slaves.[21]

Orwell's *Homage to Catalonia* was one of a number of primary sources that Ken Loach and Jim Allen consulted when making *Land and Freedom*, the significant subtitle of which – *A Story from the Spanish Revolution* – conveys their intention to work against the grain of popular history that mythologizes the events in Spain in terms of a united left crusade against fascism. Equally important, the film sets out to capture the ebullient spirit and eager commitment that helped create a profound historical experiment in self-management and collectivization. Nowhere is this more convincingly portrayed than in the long, mostly improvized, scene in which a village's farmers discuss with militants what to do with the land. In a remarkable piece of cinema, where all but two of the villagers are non-professional actors and equal weight is given to arguments and counter-arguments about whether or not to collectivize, the fluid camerawork gels flawlessly with the ebb and flow of the debate so that what comes across with verve and conviction is the willingness and ability of people to politicize their lives. What emerges too, as the villagers and the militants redraw the boundaries of what concerns them, is the realization that what constitutes the political is itself a political question. Politics as a domain inextricable from statism is questioned by the proceedings of the meeting and by its decision that social revolution cannot be indefinitely postponed while waiting for the 'right conditions'.

Land and Freedom, struggling on a budget of only £2 million, also delineates the far from simple politics of the Spanish Civil War and the role of the Communist Party. The story is told through a series of flashbacks arising from the death of David, a volunteer who has left Liverpool to fight in Spain, and his granddaughter's discovery of his letters and memorabilia. Though a member of the British Communist Party, David finds himself fighting Franco's forces in a POUM (Partido Obrero de Unificación Marxista) militia, an anti-Stalinist Marxist group that often has more in common with the anarchists than the Communist Party. He finds himself in a mixed bag of Spanish, French, Irish and American comrades, including the anarchist Bianca, with whom he meets up in Barcelona after recovering from an injury. They argue and she leaves in anger after his decision to join the Communist Party-led Popular Army. As a consequence, David finds himself taking orders from Communist-led forces to join a gun battle against the anarchist CNT holding the Barcelona telephone exchange. The battle over the exchange building, a critical assault by the Communists on the anarchists, really did take place in May 1937. So too did the smashing of the collectives by the Communist Party and the murder of anti-Stalinist communists, something that David is witness to after self-disgust makes him leave the battle for the telephone exchange and return to the POUM militia.

Land and Freedom, like *Homage to Catalonia*, draws out the fact that the Communist Party deliberately withheld arms from the anarchists and POUM, and counters the myth that militarily the libertarian and anti-Stalinist left were well-meaning but hopelessly disorganized and ill-disciplined. Moscow had nothing to gain from encouraging social revolution in Spain and, through control of the Communist Party, strangled it to death in its infancy, the realization of which leads David to tear up his Party card in bitter disillusion. *Land and Freedom* is very much a film about betrayal, but it triumphs at the same time by recreating a momentous experiment in social revolution that, almost succeeding, found an authoritarian left to be as much a hindrance as outright Fascism. Hence Loach's comment that the fog cleared in 1936 and you could see what the score was, and Jim Allen's more pointed observation that 'If you understand the lessons of Spain, then you understand the lessons of today with Tony Blair – the Social Democrats who'll always betray you.'[22] A film of under two hours cannot tell the whole story of the Spanish Civil War: it does not dwell on the anarchists' participation in regional governments and, from late in 1936, in the national Republican government under Largo Caballero. This government fell directly after the May Days of 1937 that saw the Popular Army's attack on the CNT at the telephone exchange. The CNT's participation in government remains a contentious topic and was not undertaken lightly, but in the circumstances of the time, facing the task of confronting Franco's forces while maintaining the rural collectives and other economic advances in the face of opposition from Communists and right-wing socialists, it is arguable that anarchists showed themselves to be flexible without self-destructing. After the Barcelona May Days the CNT were out of the national and Catalan governments, their control in Aragón was over and it became a struggle to maintain their influence over economic and political developments. Caballero's socialist government was replaced by a more pro-Stalinist one under Juan Negrin and orthodox command structures were imposed on the military as well as on economic affairs. As 1938 drew to a close, aid from the USSR was dwindling away, the Comintern-organized International Brigades had been withdrawn and Spanish republicans were left to face Franco.

Land and Freedom, although focusing on the rural collectives, brings to centre stage the conflict between the authoritarian Communists and the libertarian CNT and FAI. It was a major conflict, one that confirmed what had been already suggested by events in revolutionary Russia after the 1917 Revolution. The threat of a common enemy, in Russia's case invading European armies and counter-revolutionary forces and in Spain Franco's reactionary forces, provides both a rationale for authoritarian control from the centre and a soul-searching dilemma for anarchists over whether to dilute fundamental principles on the grounds of a tactical postponement. It is, essentially, the same kind of rationale used by centralized parties of the left when appealing for votes, with the conservative opposition playing the role of the common enemy. Many socialists succumb to the same old dilemma when, knowing in their hearts that the politicians they elect will probably betray them, they still cast votes in their support, forlornly hoping that something good may come of it or that a slightly left-of-centre government is better than a right-of-centre one. What happened in Spain, with whole regions setting about creating a non-hierarchical social and economic order, has lived on in the anarchist consciousness not only as a positive example of what could happen but as a warning about how centralized parties will not tolerate radical change that they cannot control.

Anarchist aspirations in Spain did not die with Franco's victory, and, for the extraordinary Sabate brothers and others, the battle was to continue through to the 1950s. When the Civil War broke out in 1936, Jose Sabate was 26, his brother Francisco 21; the youngest brother, Manuel, was only nine. The two older brothers joined their local defence group and went to the Aragón Front, and when the war was over they chose to continue the struggle from bases in the Spanish–French border region. After a series of close shaves, shoot-outs and robberies, Jose and Manuel were hunted down and killed in 1950, but Francisco returned to the fight and survived some audacious exploits and outrageous escapes before being shot down in 1960. Eric Hobsbawm portrays Francisco Sabate and his comrades as hopeless, passionate romantics, daredevil bandits, Spanish versions of Butch Cassidy and the Sundance Kid, who rationalized their passion for quixotic adventures behind the guise of political action.[23] Such an account seriously undervalues the anarchist tradition in which they made sense of their struggle. They robbed banks to finance political activities designed to raise consciousness and maintain opposition to Franco's regime, but they never harboured illusions about single-handedly overthrowing the government. One of Francisco's weapons was a home-made mortar that showered thousands of propaganda leaflets over an urban area, and in one daring bank raid he left a bomb in the doorway of a bank to deter those inside from raising the alarm. The bomb was eventually defused, revealing only sand and a note saying 'Just to show you that I am not as bloodthirsty as you make out.' The simple ardour of the Sabate brothers operated in the context of a world that now seems distant, but their remarkable lives embodied their convictions, and doubt and resignation seem rarely to have troubled their spirits.

The Spanish anarchist tradition affected people outside of Spain, like Stuart Christie who left his native Scotland as a teenager in the early 1960s with explosives in his rucksack and a desire to assassinate Franco. Arrested shortly after arriving in Spain, he was sentenced to 20 years in prison but was released after a few years and settled in London to become a gas-fitter and co-founder of Black Cross, dedicated to helping imprisoned fellow anarchists. He was later arrested in London and charged as a member of the Angry Brigade with conspiracy to cause explosions, once again facing the prospect of a lengthy prison sentence. Before this happened, however, the spectre of anarchism returned – not in Spain but on the streets of Paris.

Getting Angry

Just as the 1917 February Revolution in Russia was not planned, taking the Bolsheviks by surprise, the eruption of discontent that spread through France after student protests in Paris at the beginning of May 1968 shocked the unprepared French Communist Party and caught them with their dialectics down. Indeed, 'bound to their party, like Oedipus to his fate, [Communist students] did their utmost to stem that tide'.[24]

Beginning in mid-May, workers followed students with their own direct action as places of work were occupied; a general strike followed. The spirit of revolt has been well recorded by the likes of Daniel and Gabriel Cohn-Bendit in their first-hand description of just how close, on the night of 24 May following huge marches in support of striking workers, demonstrators in Paris came to menacing the state without recourse to arms:

> The atmosphere was electric. We then marched on the Stock Exchange as we had planned (the Hôtel de ville, another objective, was too well defended by the CRS and the army), captured it with remarkable ease and set it on fire. Paris was in the hands of the demonstrators, the revolution had started in earnest! The police could not possibly guard all the public buildings and all the strategic points: the Elysée, the Hôtel de ville, the bridges, the ORTF (the French Broadcasting Service) . . . Everyone felt it and wanted to go on. But then the political boys stepped in. It was a leader of the far-left JCR (Revolutionary Communist Youth) who in the Place de l'Opéra, took charge and turned us back towards the Latin Quarter – when most of us thought we had done with the fatal attraction of the Sorbonne. It was officers of UNEF [National Union of French Students] and PSU [United Socialist Party] who stopped us taking the Ministry of Finance and the Ministry of Justice. These 'revolutionaries' were quite incapable of grasping the potential of a movement that had left them far behind and was still gaining momentum. As for us, we failed to realize how easy it would have been to sweep all these nobodies away . . . It is now clear that if, on 25 May, Paris had woken to find the most important Ministries occupied, Gaullism would have caved in at once – the more so as similar actions would have taken place all over the country.[25]

Although the Communist Party had gained a leadership role in much left-wing dissent in post-World War II France, the student demonstrators of May '68 had broken free of this and were keenly aware of the danger that a centralist, statist Communist Party posed to the chances of a libertarian revolution. Behind its prankish sense of glee, the telegram sent to the Communist Party of the USSR by the Occupation Committee of the Sorbonne showed their sense of history:

```
SHAKE IN YOUR SHOES BUREAUCRATS STOP THE INTER-
NATIONAL POWER OF THE WORKERS' COUNCILS WILL
SOON WIPE YOU OUT STOP HUMANITY WILL NOT BE
HAPPY UNTIL THE LAST BUREAUCRAT IS HUNG WITH
THE GUTS OF THE LAST CAPITALIST STOP LONG LIVE
THE STRUGGLE OF THE KRONSTADT SAILORS AND OF
THE MAKHNOVSCHINA AGAINST TROTSKY AND LENIN
STOP LONG LIVE THE 1956 COUNCILIST INSURRECTION
OF BUDAPEST STOP DOWN WITH THE STATE STOP
```

In the end, the anarchist spirit and near-revolutionary turmoil of events in Paris in 1968 petered out and the brief student–worker alliance it gave birth to was smothered in a political deal negotiated between Communist Party-led trade unionists and the government. The eruption of May '68 could not be directly linked to a crisis in the economy, and it was only later that the Party and trade union leaders turned the uprising into a set of negotiations about wages. While it lasted, though, the spectre of an anarchist-inspired revolt had threatened to tear a rip in the West's Cold War political order, and the reverberations of the event were not to be quietened as smoothly as the brokers of powers might have wished. One example of the aftershock is reflected in the work of French filmmakers like Jean-Luc Godard and Jean-Pierre Gorin, most notably when they came to make *Tout va bien* two years later. One can only imagine what might have happened in France if the trade union movement, instead of being led by bureaucrats and members of the Communist Party, had borne some resemblance to the FAI and CNT of Spain.

Some of those who found themselves charged with the Angry Brigade campaign in Britain in the 1970s had experienced the revolutionary spirit that swept over Paris in 1968, and a French connection marked the inauspicious beginning to the Brigade's symbolic bombing crusade in 1970, when a small package containing two cartridges of French explosive failed to explode at the site of a new police station in Paddington, London. Three months later, a series of three bombs did explode and two of them were at the homes of Establishment figures, although the facts were hushed up by the authorities and went unreported in the media. The target of the next bomb, when four ounces of TNT exploded under an empty BBC transmission van, was a Miss World contest the BBC was filming. This was 19 November 1970, and on 4 December a burst of machine-gun fire hit the Spanish Embassy in London. Five days later the target was the offices of the Ministry of Employment in London, on a day when trade unionists were holding a major demonstration against new legislation that would allow for trade unions to be punished financially for strikes and for individual trade unionists to be imprisoned for unofficial industrial disputes. In January 1971 another explosion wrecked the front door of the home of the Home Secretary, then a fashion boutique was attacked, followed by an attempt to blow up London's police computer. The homes of the managing director of the car company Ford and another government minister were also damaged by bomb attacks. Since the days of the Angry Brigade, the devastating use of non-symbolic bombing campaigns by various non-anarchist groups around the world makes it difficult to appreciate the fact that the Angry Brigade were not serious bombers, in the sense that we now understand the term. It is also difficult to take into account the fact that at the time the Conservative government was seen to be cracking down on organized working-class opposition to free-market capitalism, which it was, and the Angry Brigade saw their campaign as a part of this opposition.

On 20 August, two couples in their early 20s were arrested in their north London flat at 359 Amhurst Rd, Stoke Newington, and John Barker, Hilary Creek, Jim Greenfield and Anna Mendelson were charged with conspiracy to cause explosions. When Stuart Christie turned up at the flat the following day he was arrested and charged, the police claiming that two detonators were in the boot of his car. Also arrested, and facing the same trial that was to follow, were Chris Bott, Angie Weir and Kate McLean, a group that came to be known as the Stoke Newington Eight. The police claimed to have found ammunition, guns, and 33 sticks of gelignite in the flat.

Mendelson, Barker and Creek chose to defend the themselves in court and the defendants as a whole did not disown the Angry Brigade, arguing and insisting instead that they were being framed by the police. Those defending themselves made no secret of their political and social convictions, referring to subjects ranging from old people dying of cold in sub-standard housing to internment in Northern Ireland. A leading police officer who described the campaign as one of violence and anarchy told the court in reply to a question that he was not aware that ten people die a week in industrial accidents. The case against Bott, Weir and McLean was weak from the very start, while the case against Christie and the four from Amhurst Road could only collapse if it was believed the police had framed the defendants. This was 1972, years before the convictions of people for IRA bombings in Britain would be shown to have resulted from police malpractice. Nevertheless, the jury failed to reach a unanimous decision and it seems they finally reached a compromise majority decision by agreeing to convict Mendelson, Barker, Creek and Greenfield while acquitting the others of all the charges against them. Two of the jurors did not change their minds about finding all eight defendants innocent. Although the four from Amhurst Road were found guilty, the jury made an unprecedented plea to the judge for clemency to be shown towards those they had just convicted. They were sentenced to ten years, instead of the fifteen years that Jake Prescott had received in an earlier, separate trial that found him guilty of addressing some of the envelopes carrying Angry Brigade communiqués.

The police never uncovered any new facts about the Angry Brigade campaign and the eight people who spent the summer of 1972 in the Old Bailey dock have remained broadly silent on the subject.[26] Four more bombings took place after the arrests, the most spectacular of which occurred at the top of London's Post Office Tower at the end of October 1971. The final bombing took place two days later, totalling over 20 Angry Brigade bombings in all, plus six devices that failed to explode. In no cases were members of the public killed or seriously injured; one person received a minor injury.

What is clear is that the Angry Brigade did not see itself as a vanguard for the revolution, and their small-scale bombs were never designed to kill or maim. Many of the attacks were designed to complement the industrial unrest that characterized Britain in the early 1970s, a period when the government was determined to rein in workers' discontent by means of repressive legislation. It is also clear that the Angry Brigade emerged from a network of radical activists that were involved in various social issues like homelessness and the women's movement. A guide to the motives and make-up of the Angry Brigade is to be found in the language of the communiqués that were issued. Communiqué 1 was brief and self-explanatory though the mention of spectacles, a key term from French Situationist theory, may have flummoxed the British police:

```
          Fascism & oppression
             will be smashed
    Embassies                    (Spanish Emb
    Judges                              Machine gunned
    High Pigs                     Thursday)
    Spectacles
    Property

                             Communique 1
                             The Angry Brigade²⁷
```

Communiqué 5, released after a bombing in January 1971, confirmed what
had already become clear, namely that targets were being selected for their
symbolic value: 'We are no mercenaries. We attack property not people.
Carr, Rawlinson, Waldron [those whose homes had been bombed] would
all be dead if we had wished.' Communiqué 7 consists of a longer statement, and its language suggests that the Angry Brigade was not fresh out of
the Marxist-Leninist mould of revolutionary politics:

```
Look at the barriers . . . don't breathe . . . don't
love . . . don't strike, don't make trouble . . .
DON'T. The politicians, the leaders, the rich, the big
bosses are in command . . . THEY CONTROL. WE, THE PEOPLE,
SUFFER . . . THEY have tried to make us mere functions
of a production process. THEY have polluted the world
with chemical waste from their factories. THEY shoved
garbage from their media down our throats. THEY made
us absurd sexual caricatures, all of us, men and
women . . . There is a certain kind of professional
who claims to represent us . . . the M.P.s, the
Communist Party, the Union leaders, the Social
Workers, the old-old left . . . All these people
presumed to act on our behalf. All these people have
certain things in common . . . THEY always sell us out.
```

A libertarian note, merging the private with the political, is struck in the opening sentence and the statement expresses the anarchist belief that the hierarchical power structures of traditional communist and left-wing parties and trade unions will work against the interests of those they claim to represent. Similar anarchist sentiments appeared in the communiqué of October 1971: 'Without any Central Committee and no hierarchy to classify our members, we can only know strange faces as friends through their actions. We love them – we embrace them – as we know others will.' At the same time, though, the language of some of the communiqués also suggests a familiarity with Marxist-Leninist discourse, like the declaration in Communiqué 6 that 'Our role is to deepen the political contradictions at every level' and the promise to continue a bombing campaign 'until, armed, the revolutionary working class overthrows the capitalist system'. At other times the language veers away from the directly political and targets consumer culture in the style of Paris '68: 'Life is so boring, there's nothing to do except spend all our wages on the latest skirt or shirt. Brothers and sisters, what are your real desires?' The rhetorical and theatrical style of the communiqués helped the broadsheet newspapers dismiss Angry Brigade members as revolutionary pollyannas, but their anger was sincere and justified. Frustrated by the power structure within the legitimate options that were open to them, like trade unions and left-wing political parties, and wanting to take direct action and make a difference they became angry, gave expression to it, and hoped the feeling would spread: 'The Angry Brigade is the man or woman next to you. They have guns in their pockets and anger in their minds.' Perhaps the impatient Angry Brigade campaign was too gestural for its own good, distracting attention from the other kind of campaigns that many of the Stoke Newington Eight had been a part of, but the anger and love that sustained it is not qualitatively that different from the passion and determination of the anti-capitalist movement.

Somewhere between the anger in their minds and the guns in their pockets was a thin line that tried to balance the symbolic value of violence as an expression of political anger with physical violence itself. The use of political violence in anarchist activities comes from the tradition of direct action, and while this tradition does not necessarily endorse violence, it has a history of using violence. This tradition goes back to Bakunin and propaganda by the deed, and the anarchism in Italy in the 1870s when a strategy of guerrilla propaganda was developed. A band of anarchists would mount an insurrection in one town, demonstrate what could be done and then, having roused class consciousness, leave the inhabitants to take it from there. Such a programme started, abortively, at Bologna in 1874 and three years later at San Lupo, where a group of anarchists marched to the village of Letino distributing weapons and tax collectors' receipts. There was a positive response from one village, though not from another, and they were later captured while trying to escape. Part of the appeal of such direct action comes from the expectation that consciousness can be raised through a symbolic act of violence. The act of violence is seen as a primer that might set off a wave of popular discontent, a precondition for a meaningful insurrection. Anarchism's emphasis on the individual encourages personal revolt, direct action in response to a particular situation. Anarchist acts of this kind came to the fore in France and elsewhere in the early 1890s, largely carried out by disparate individuals who thereby gave birth to the stereotype of the insurrectionist carrying a spherical bomb with a fuse, and climaxing with the assassination of French President Carnot in 1894. Not all of these actions were as politically directed as the death of Carnot and a bomb at a Barcelona theatre in 1893 that killed 20 people, the kind of act Malatesta may have had in mind when he wrote a last entry in a notebook the day before he died in 1923: 'He who throws a bomb and kills a pedestrian, declares that as a victim of society he has rebelled against society. But could not the poor victim object: "Am I Society?"'[28]

The Angry Brigade had no intention of killing people as a result of their bombings, but it was easy for the media to downplay this. It was possible to conflate the Angry Brigade, as terrorists, with the German Red Army Faction (RAF) of the 1970s. Members of the RAF were urban guerrillas who declared class war on the state, robbed banks, shot policemen and soldiers, exploded bombs, organized hijackings and took hostages. The extreme commitment to direct action displayed by the likes of Ulrike Meinhof, who died in prison in 1976, and Andreas Baader, Gudrun Ensslin and Jan Carl Raspe who later also died in prison, led to anarchist interest in their actions. Many anarchists could empathise with the RAF's resolve to confront the state, and for some they represented a possible mode of resistance. Some of the early communiqués from the Red Army Faction, like the concluding lines of this one from May 1972, do not sound very different to those of the Angry Brigade:

> We will carry out bomb attacks against judges and public prosecutors until they have stopped abusing the rights of political prisoners . . . Freedom for political prisoners! Fight class justice! Fight fascism![29]

Despite a passing family resemblance, the Red Army Faction was not an anarchist organization and the historical background out of which the RAF emerged was very specific to the West Germany of the Cold War period. It was a time when West Germany was firmly cemented in the grip of US power, just as East Germany was in USSR power. The Vietnam War was on and American bases in West Germany were tangible evidence of the US intention to prosecute militarily the perceived threat of Communist ambitions. Such a perceived threat also became an excuse to ensure that radical left-wing opposition within West Germany was suppressed. There was no political space in the West German state for legitimate opposition to the way things were, and the radicals that became known as the Baader-Meinhof group were reacting to this extreme situation in an extreme way. An early recorded statement by Gudrun Ensslin came in response to the police killing of a student in West Berlin during a demonstration against the visit of the Shah of Iran, at the time a pro-American player in the Cold War. The statement reveals something of the historical consciousness that haunted the RAF, an essential part of their hatred of the state and capitalism:

> They'll kill us all. You know what kind of pigs we're up against.This is the Auschwitz generation we've got against us. You can't argue with the people who made Auschwitz. They have weapons and we haven't. We must arm ourselves.[30]

The RAF situated its theory and practice within a Leninist tradition, finding in Lenin a correct analysis of the international struggle they saw themselves as a part of, but the language of the group makes clear they were not a mainstream Leninist party. In 1972, when incendiary bombs were exploded in two of Frankfurt's largest department stores as a protest against the Vietnam War, capitalism and imperialism were the target but the explanation for the action was unusual: 'We set fires in the department stores so that you will stop buying. The compulsion to buy terrorises you', stated Ensslin.[31] There is also an anarchist flavour to the angry denunciation of the modern capitalist state that formed part of an early RAF statement:

> Those who don't defend themselves die. Those who don't die are buried in prisons, in reform schools, in the slums of workers' districts, in the stone coffins of the new housing developments, in the crowded kindergartens and schools, in the brand new kitchens and bedrooms filled with furniture bought on credit.[32]

At the same time, though, the following description of revolutionary activity by Ulrike Meinhof is rooted in the tradition of the October Revolution: 'The guerrilla is a cadre organization, the aim of its collective learning process is the equality of the fighters, the collectivisation of each one, enabling them to analyse and to practice independence and to acquire the ability to create an armed nucleus, and to keep open the collective learning process.' [33] The RAF gave Bolshevism a modern edge, fusing thought and action, being and becoming, in an anarchistic dance brought to heel by the ontological dictate of history: 'Everything is constantly in motion, as is the struggle. Struggle comes out of motion, moving on. The struggle is moving on. All that matters is the aim. The Guerrilla perceives class struggle as the basic principle of history and class struggle as the reality in which proletarian politics will be realized.' [34] The Bolshevism of the RAF placed it outside the history of anarchism, but the anger and the commitment of the Baader-Meinhof group tapped into an anarchist tradition of conspiratorial direct action that goes back to Bakunin and his futile plots to bring down governments in revolutionary acts that would set off a mass upheaval.

You Can't Blow Up a Social Relationship, but . . .

There is an alternative anarchist tradition of non-violence, one that goes back to the pacifism of Tolstoy and the direct action *satyagraha* campaign of Gandhi. *Satyagraha*, from two Gujarati words meaning 'truth' and 'force', provided Gandhi with a doctrine of non-violent resistance as the basis for a campaign of social struggle. The *satyagraha* was to serve Gandhi's vision of a post-independent India that would not replicate the hierarchies of control that had facilitated British rule. Independence from Britain was not an end in itself, and in this sense Gandhi was not a nationalist. Declaring himself an anarchist on more than once occasion, Gandhi sought to avoid the centralized utopias of authoritarian socialism.

The caste system was only the most visible form of a society that divided power unequally, and Gandhi opposed the religious cleavage between Hindu and Muslim from the same commitment to the building of a society without social or religious discriminations. Gandhi's practical proposals for change in rural village life were designed to prepare the way for communal reconciliation and the nurturing of economic autonomy through localization. His vision of a liberated India was not a primitivist one but it was anarchistic. 'The State', he says, 'represents violence in a concentrated and organized form',[35] and a rural-based, decentralized economic system was envisaged as an alternative way of organizing production. In the political sphere, Gandhi rejected the parliamentary system in favour of a federation of elected officials administering a decentralized and demilitarized state: 'self-government means continuous effort to be free of government control, whether it is foreign or whether it is national.' [36] *Satyagraha* and Gandhi's programme for social and political rejuvenation overlaps in places with the anti-capitalist movement and its broad commitment to non-violence and its espousal of localization against the power of multi-nationals. For many, non-violence is not a matter of strategy or tactics, and numerous anarchists share Gandhi's conviction that the principle objection to violence comes from the nature of the relationship between ends and means. Unless society as a whole sees and feels the need for an alternative, there is no good reason to try and forcibly impose one because such an approach will be necessarily at odds with the *raison d'etre* of anarchism. This realization was enshrined in the title of a pamphlet by an anonymous group of Australian anarchists, *You Can't Blow Up a Social Relationship*. It is a strand of anarchism that has re-emerged in the anti-capitalist movement, based on the realization that the means and the ends can not be separated, that anarchism *realizes* itself in its forms of organization and action. The ideal of a peaceful, non-capitalist society cannot be worked towards in any meaningfully way other than by a commitment to non-violent change.

Rubbing up against the obvious truth that you can't explode with a bomb the social relationships and hierarchies of capitalism is another truth that seems equally obvious to most anarchists. Namely, that unless some effective action is undertaken, the present state of affairs remains essentially unchanged. The anarchist tradition of direct action, fuelled by anger at the way things are and a determination to make a difference, lends itself to a confrontational approach that raises thorny issues about violence and social change. Just as there is a tension within anarchism between anarcho-communism and individualism there is also a tension between a commitment to pacifism and a belief that violence is quite likely to be an unavoidable consequence of calls for radical social change. 'Normal' police violence at Seattle escalated at the anti-capitalist protest in Gothenburg in June 2001 to the issuing of live ammunition to the police, with three people shot. When another anti-capitalist protest was mounted in Genoa in July, the event turned into a violent riot, with armoured vans driving at speed into crowds of protestors and a late-night, cold-blooded and very violent assault by the police on a building where media activists and their material were lodged. For some of those at Genoa, while fully accepting that the Italian police were spoiling for a fight, the event became a riot because Black Bloc anarchists adopted violent methods, premeditatedly attacking banks and other buildings, which then allowed the authorities to assault all the demonstrators. From another point of view, it was the premeditated violence of the Italian state that was significant, showing that the police were under orders not to allow a Seattle-like protest to disrupt the Summit, and the smashing of bank windows was a red herring in terms of the state's determination to crush dissent, demonize peaceful demonstrators and deter future protest. In the introduction to what is the best written account of what took place in Genoa, activists defend their action by saying violence is too strong a word to describe their militancy: 'it's a word that should be reserved for our enemies. Our violence is a drop in the ocean when compared to their violence. We prefer to call it a confrontational approach.'[37] By gathering in large numbers and with the stated intention of trying to get inside the Red Zone, the area cordoned-off with 20-foot-high fences, the protestors were confronting the state with direct action. Is it naïve to believe that if none of the protest groups had engaged in any kind of 'mindful destruction',[38] then there would have been no violence on the part of the police? Or, to put the same question in broader terms, is it possible to effectively confront the state without accepting the probable inevitability of a violent response by the authorities? Pacifist anarchists could point to Gandhi's campaign in India and argue that, Yes, if a movement is strong and large enough then it is possible to take on the state. Others would argue that the complex situation in India at the time cannot be simplistically used as a paradigm case in this kind of argument. It ignores the fact, for instance, that the British, far from making concessions *because* of Gandhi's pacifism, were able to use his campaign for their own ends. More generally, many anarchists want to insist that pacifism cannot adequately deal with the fact that violence will be used by the state to defend its class interests.

A group that has given a most trenchant expression to anarchism's rejection of the pacifist left is the Class War Federation that emerged in 1985, from groups formed in London and elsewhere earlier in that decade. Early issues of their publication, *Class War*, urged its readers to fight back at a personal level, reversing Gandhi's precept 'Hate the sin but not the sinner':

> For far too long we've been taking a hammering and the rich have been getting away with it. They're winning the class war and they aren't even taking any causalities. They live it up under our very noses . . . We've got to fight vicious and nasty instead of normal political activity – boring marches, petitions etc . . . We must make our anger and hatred personal. 'Smash the system' and other dickhead slogans of the left have no reality. The system has

no real existence outside of individuals, there is no Capitalism without Capitalists. Even when we destroy their property the insurance companies just cough up for it. We must switch our attack to areas where they are not so easily protected. Let them know what it's like to be on the receiving end for a change.[39]

Class War brought a fresh, punk quality to class consciousness and urged readers to express their anger by harassing the rich:

> press your faces against the restaurant windows where these bloated shitbags are stuffing themselves – put them off their meal . . . Fuck getting 250,000 people to tramp like sheep through London to listen to middle-class C.N.D. wankers . . . Let's just get 5,000 to turn up at Ascot or the Henley Regatta and let our class anger loose on them. Get them when they're hunting. Instead of spraying aniseed at the hounds, drag the master of the hunt off his horse and give him a good kicking. The locals will be happy at the sight of the local squire being carted off to hospital.[40]

Bash the Rich events did take place, though some of the Class War 'leaders' stirring up direct action of this kind were canny enough not to wade in themselves with boots flying. Surprising to some, Class War began to get noticed and circulation soared to the giddy heights of 15,000 with a refreshing diet of tabloid-style headlines ('Labour Party – A Bunch of Tossers', 'Rich Bastards Beware', 'Why I Hate the Rich') backed up by astute criticism of traditional socialism and the way representative forms of political organization translate into the control of political participation and the diffusion of class anger. The development of the politics of the Class War Federation only became apparent to a wider public with the publication in 1992 of their *Unfinished Business*,[41] an incisive analysis of contemporary Britain from a coherent anarchist perspective.

The Class War Federation and its spiky newspaper invigorated anarchism in Britain, and *Unfinished Business* was a coherent reply to the criticism that it championed an outmoded notion of the working class. *Class War* was not published for the chattering class of socialists, or armchair libertarian socialists for that matter, and it deliberately antagonized middle-class radicals by only addressing itself to an audience of dispossessed, working-class people living in council house estates and coping with poorly paid, unfulfilling jobs. *Class War* was also misunderstood by middle-class radicals who failed to tune in to the rhetorical excess of the newspaper, an excess that was essential to its energy and verve. The style and format of *Class War* aped the tabloid style of *The Sun*, and the paper's gleeful eulogizing of violence was presented in just this way. Anyone reading issues of *Class War* could have been forgiven for thinking that hitting a policeman over the head with a brick was the best, if not the only, way to advance the course of social change. Remarkably, though, members of the Class War Federation came to question this tendency to make a fetish of violence and the group's propensity to play up to their macho, anti-intellectual image. It began to concern thoughtful members of the Federation that they were enjoying notoriety at the expense of advancing their politics and attracting a wider membership, including women, who were especially turned off by the over-emphasis on violence. Self-criticism and a painfully honest analysis of its own holier-than-thou politics led to a split within the Class War Federation, climaxing with the final issue of *Class War* in the summer of 1997 and its headline '*Class War* is Dead . . . Long Live the Class War'. Astonishingly good to read, this final issue of the newspaper addressed the group's strengths and weaknesses and concluded that it was time to self-destruct and move on. It was recognized that the globalization of capitalism had implications for the way class struggle should be understood, and the Class War Federation also admitted that anarchists, far from honestly engaging with the challenge of trying to change the world, can complacently cocoon themselves within their own self-righteous zeal: 'We are not interested in anarchism as a hobby or as a way of being superior to others who haven't yet had the good sense to become anarchists themselves.'[42]

The recognition that the line dividing violence from non-violence will be decided on by the state, and the acknowledgement that at some stage violence may become inevitable, remains an important dimension to contemporary anarchism. At the same time, the success of the anti-capitalist movement, and in particular the development of the Zapatista National Liberation Army (EZLN), has moved the argument on, and perhaps decisively so. The Zapatista insurrection began on New Year's Day 1994,[43] when some 2,000 armed insurgents occupied towns and a city in Chiapas, the southernmost state of Mexico. Declaring war on the national government, they called for self-determination for the indigenous peoples and peasants of the Chiapas region, and their socialist rhetoric misled the Mexico government into caricaturing the Zapatistas as another bunch of Central American Marxist guerrillas. It soon became clear that the Zapatista uprising was something else, something very new – the first post-Cold War rebellion, and one that felt no need to align itself with old-style Marxist ideology. Instead, it called on all Mexicans to show solidarity with the indigenous people of Chiapas, asserting that it had no agenda for a Marxist-style reorganization of society and no wish to seize power. Appealing to a world-wide audience, groups were invited to monitor the Zapatista armed revolt.

EZLN began its revolutionary existence in a hierarchical mode familiar to rural, Maoist-inclined guerrillas and it was the result of their interaction with the various Mayan language and ethnic groups of Chiapas, the *indigenas*, that their centralized command structure was questioned and found wanting. By the time of the rebellion in 1994, the EZLN had become the Zapatista movement, with no leadership, no executive body, no headquarters. Such a form came from the life of the *indigenas*, based on ideas of community and communal decision making:

the *indigenas* did not consider themselves to be sovereign individuals in a society but organic members of a community. They argued for hours and hours, entire nights, for months and months, before arriving at what they called *the agreement*. On reaching the agreement, those who were against it had no option; either they followed along with the rest, or they left the community.[44]

A mutual process of education in the 1980s between the indigenous people of Chiapas and the EZLN resulted in the formulation of a new revolutionary agenda, one that modified the EZLN's Maoist-style notion of the rural guerrilla and led in 1994 to the Zapatistas declaring that they were not interested in seizing political power. The Mexican state was being opposed because it was a state and, in its stead, a participatory democracy was sought that would allow citizens to challenge the economic order. The *indigenas* of Chiapas, always one of the poorest and class-divided regions of Mexico, suffered especially as a result of the neoliberal policies of the central government, and Subcomandante Insurgente Marcos, who emerged as a remarkably eloquent spokesperson for the rebels, remarked in 1995 how Zapatista had realized that the road to self-determination no longer followed the traditional route of opposition to a national government: 'When we rose up against a national government, we found that it did not exist. In reality we were up against great financial capital, against speculation and investment, which made all decisions in Mexico, as well as in Europe, Asia, Africa, Oceania, the Americas – everywhere.'[45] The realization was accompanied by a realignment of its own politics, as the Zapatistas continued to press for radical land reform but widened its constituency and sought a peaceful settlement, confronted gender and sexual issues and pressed for 'globalization from below' by insisting on decentralized forms of government.

The development of the Zapatista uprising owes a great deal to the nature of the support it received during and after 1994. This support was not military (despite calls for other indigenous group to rebel), but came in the form of activists from a variety of backgrounds – human rights, indigenous rights, peace groups, environmentalists – that were able to wire in via the new media, with some travelling to Chiapas and organizing a medley of support groups and *ad hoc* activities. As a result the Zapatista movement became more amorphous and less militaristic, and in August 1996 the movement hosted the International Encounter for Humanity and Against Neoliberalism, attended by 3,000 delegates from nearly 50 countries, giving birth to the anti-capitalist movement.

In its own small way, an anarchist-minded group in Copenhagen has been making a practical contribution to what remains the long-term aim of Zapatista and the anti-capitalist movement as a whole: the building of a global civil society to oppose global capitalism and the power of the state. The 'free city' of Christiania came into existence over 30 years ago, when activists began moving into a site of abandoned military buildings and set about creating an alternative way of living. Over the years Christiania has experienced some tumultuous encounters with state authorities, from exasperated officials demanding taxes to invasion by brigades of riot-suited police. Divided into fifteen districts, Christiania is home and workplace to between 650 and 1,000 people living in buildings they have mostly designed and constructed themselves. The area is free of government taxes, though residents and businesses pay rents to the community's Common Funds. This covers necessary expenses like the collection and disposal of garbage, children's facilities, electricity and water costs. The fifteen local areas have their own Area Funds.

More so than in the *polis* of classical Athens, government is fully democratic, and all major decisions are reached at open meetings to which everyone residing in Christiania is invited. When a general meeting is in progress, the shops and cafés close down and discussion of items on the agenda continues until a consensus is reached. Decisions are not made on the basis of voting and, consequently, some decisions are not quickly arrived at. The fifteen administrative and autonomous districts hold their own monthly meetings, and contact groups are formed by district representatives as and when the need arises.

Christiania is not to be imagined in terms of an anarchist idyll and, politically, the place is no more homogenous than was the ancient Athenian *polis*. In total, only about 20 per cent of the residents share what could loosely be called an anarchist perspective, and they share living space with citizens of all political persuasions. Conservatives live in Christiania, cycle off to work in the city wearing suits and have little truck with the more public face of Christiania. The soft-drug dealers on Pusher Street are as hard-nosed a bunch as one would expect and, now an official 'social experiment', Christiania has become a major tourist attraction for visitors intrigued by the prospect of an alternative lifestyle flourishing in the heart of a modern bourgeois state. At the same time though, the anarchist districts of Christiania are genuinely alternative and, as one might expect, there is a range of opinion amongst the mix of older, traditional libertarians and direct-action militants. There are a small number of anarchist collectives that share everything in common and some refuse to use electricity as part of their endeavour to live outside of the state. Propaganda by the deed has always been a part of the anarchist tradition and districts like Björnekloen, Blå Karamel and South Dyssen have given it a new meaning.

Over three centuries separate the Diggers' communist community at St George's Hill in England from Christiania's bold and enduring social experiment in Denmark, but there is a connecting pattern of thought and a shared resolve to put into effect libertarian practices of an anarchist nature. Winstanley, like the Christianites, hoped to demonstrate that people were capable of running their own lives by working cooperatively; and while the programme for a communist utopia at St George's Hill only managed to survive twelve months, Christiania has been functioning for over 30 years. In that time they have built houses, schools, playgrounds, opened shops and restaurants, galvanized social awareness, hosted some memorable musical events, run a variety of cooperatives, established recycling programmes and wind and solar power projects, and developed a participatory form of direct democracy and administration of financial funds and communal resources. As with the Diggers, there have been conflicts and collisions with state powers along the way, although the challenge now facing Christiania is to keep alive the libertarian spirit and practice that motivated the first generation of rebels.

Anarchism's attack on the state has indeed taken many forms, from bullets, bombs and Bash the Rich stunts to the poetic politics of the Zapatistas and do-it-yourself activists of Christiania. The contemporary anti-capitalist movement brings together many of these forms, although the bullets are now being provided by state forces and not by anarchists.

CHAPTER FIVE

Subverting Hierarchies

Wheels in the Head

In an important sense, the difference between liberals and anarchists is one of depth. Liberals, including socialists, like to imagine that piecemeal changes, albeit radical ones when necessary, can put the machinery of state on a sane basis. Exploitation can be reduced and minimized through enlightened legislation by way of political parties with the necessary will to realize their progressive agendas. Anarchism, far from being at odds with liberal values, understands the depth of change that is necessary to meaningfully implement them for everyone, and works towards that end. Anarchism subjects the existing order to a deeper and more sustained analysis than liberalism and identifies the mechanisms and thought patterns, social and psychological as well as political and economic, by which exploitation and class control are maintained. In its concern with issues of authority, command and domination, anarchism seeks to understand why people accept class exploitation, why more people do not rebel.

At times in the past, anarchism's radical dissent has become largely associated with attacks directed at state institutions and the authority of governments, yet the anarchist's opposition to imposed authority, hierarchical forms of power and all forms of domination has developed in areas of thought well beyond the narrowly political. It is especially clear to anarchists that the existing order is rooted in the control of social life and that the acceptance of certain attitudes, reinforced through structures of authority and obedience, makes up a state of intellectual imprisonment which in some of its aspects takes on forms of psychic repression – what Max Stirner called 'wheels in the head'.[1]

It doesn't follow, by any means, that individuals or groups opposed to authoritarianism are honorary anarchists, but there are a number of movements, cultural formations and sensibilities, as well as individuals, who explore and oppose 'non-political' forms of authoritarianism and hierarchical structures in sufficiently coherent ways as to endear them to anarchists, if they are not already self-consciously situated within the anarchist tradition. Modes of thought that undermine attitudes and structures premised on notions of authority and obedience are as vital to the libertarian left as are more traditional concerns with political organizations and institutions. Far from evading the need to address questions of political control, the concern with cultural and social issues based around ideas of authority and obedience is based on a broader understanding of how political power is maintained. It springs from the realization that the capture of political power is not necessarily the primary act. To think in terms of 'capturing' or 'winning' political power, and the containment of theory within like-minded terms, employs a simplistic and misleading subject–object approach to the possibility of radical change. The alternative to this way of thinking is not to evade the fact that ruling classes do not voluntarily hand over power, as if revolution can happily motor along on a fuel of high-octane enthusiasm, but to understand why more people do not revolt and why so many submit to structures of authority that make them unhappy. Coming to such an understanding is just as important as building up organized resistance. In particular, anarchism is concerned with the effects of alienation, not just in the workplace but in the social being of people's daily lives, and this helps explain the relevance and appeal of Situationism.

Situationism, associated with the 1960s and, in particular, the Paris revolt in May 1968, was anchored in a Cold War context, one that sought a re-interpretation of traditional Marxism. The emergence of the New Left, allied to a fresh re-emergence of anarchist ideas in left-wing intellectual circles, provides a broad background to the Janus-faced Situationism that looked back to modernism while unwittingly glancing forwards to forms of urban anarchism. In between was Situationism's precocious awareness of how the revolutionary dynamic of capitalism – that which Marx gave breathless expression to in *The Communist Manifesto* – had entered a new phase. Under this new aspect, oppression came not from dark Satanic mills but from the likes of advertising, architecture, tourism, supermarkets and superstars. Capitalism was anything but conservative, it could humanize the commodity, mine illicit and subconscious desires and colonize the avant-garde while cementing the essentials of the class system behind a trance of sensuous and seemingly satisfying consumption.

Marx, describing the consequences of the transition from feudalism to capitalism, wrote of how the 'heavenly ecstasies of religious fervour, of chivalrous enthusiasm, of philistine sentimentalism' had been drowned in 'the icy water of egotistical calculation'.[2] In its new phase, however, capitalism could audaciously present commodities as objects of desire that recaptured aspects of what Marx thought had been destroyed. Situationism, recognizing this, sought a counter move based on the fact that alienation could not so easily be abolished, however subtle the mediation, and that revolt could be provoked through *détournement*, a subversive misappropriation of the images, symbols and artefacts that so cannily disguise the metaphysical poverty of a class-based, consumer society.

The Situationist International, founded in 1957 by a small group of European intellectuals and avant-garde artists, sought to challenge the passive consumer culture that they identified as a new form of alienation. As early as 1953, in the third issue of *Lettrist International*, the publication of a Paris-based group that would co-establish the Situationist International four years later, a dissonant note is heard in the voice of Guy Debord declaring, 'At no price do we want to participate, to accept keeping quiet, to accept. It's not out of arrogance that it displeases us to resemble everyone else.'[3] The Situationist International went on to address a need to bring to light 'forgotten desires', a need which would be facilitated by the creation of 'situations' (hence the group's name) that would invite citizens to become playful participants in life rather than passive observers of the 'spectacle'.[4] The spectacle was the Situationist's versatile term for the commodification of modern capitalist society, suggesting mere show, a representation, in which the consumer adopts an audience mentality. For Situationism, clearly influenced by Dadaism in this respect, art itself has become part of this show, part of a cultural wasteland created by a functional logic that served only the interests of the ruling bourgeoisie. The highpoint of notoriety for the Situationists came when the publication of a Situationist pamphlet, 'On the Poverty of Student Life', at Strasbourg University in 1966 led to a court order closing down the student union. When Paris did erupt a year and a half later, the Situationist International claimed a role in the insurrection stemming from the influence of this pamphlet.

While the Situationist International did not consciously align itself with the anarchist movement,[5] it was well aware of the anarchist influence on Dadaism and Surrealism and of political anarchism as a whole. The nature and purpose of the spectacle, its invitation to passively consume, was seen to be imbricated in a political order that depended on a hierarchical, class-based society. Debord saw the spectacle as consumer capitalism's advance on fetishism and reification. The spectacle was not so much a specific object or image, but the social relations between people fabricated by the images of a spectacular society. This is not just consumerism; people themselves can form a spectacle, raising alienation to a new, lived level of objectification.

Paradoxically, while explicitly defining itself as a non-hierarchical movement, Situationist International suffered from a clique mentality and indulged in periodic bouts of exclusions and resignations worthy of any sodden Marxist-Leninist splinter group. At the same time, the group had the ability to offer provocative interpretations that went beyond anything traditional parties of the left could come up with. The 1962 Situationist analysis of the Paris Commune of 1871, for instance, celebrated the leaderless and carnivalesque nature of the event in a way that forecast the festive eruption in Paris of 1968.[6] During the early 1960s, when the group was active, there was no shortage of aspirations and much-vaunted endeavours, but little was purposefully followed through, unless the decapitation of the Little Mermaid statue in Copenhagen harbour is regarded as an inspiring release of 'forgotten desires'. The Situationists though, notwithstanding their elitism, are justly remembered for their subversive programme and the creative impetus they provided for graffiti artists in Paris in 1968. Many of the famous slogans that appeared –

BE REALISTIC, DEMAND THE IMPOSSIBLE

IT IS FORBIDDEN TO FORBID

TAKE YOUR DESIRES FOR REALITY

THE COMMODITY IS THE OPIUM OF THE PEOPLE

THE MORE YOU CONSUME THE LESS YOU LIVE

ART IS DEAD: DO NOT CONSUME ITS CORPSE

NEVER WORK

RUN, COMRADE, THE OLD WORLD IS BEHIND YOU

UNDER THE PAVING STONES, THE BEACH

– if not directly inspired by anarcho-Situationist texts, were certainly in harmony with its spirit of insubordination.

There are direct links between Situationism and other more avowedly anarchist groups of the 1960s. A former Situationist became one of the early activists in the Dutch Provos, an anarchist group that emerged in Amsterdam in 1965, and one of the originators of Kommune 1 in Berlin around the same time was also a former Situationist. It was the Dutch Provos who launched a propaganda attack on private property in the summer of 1965 by making white painted bicycles freely available in the capital – only to have them confiscated by the authorities – and who the following year launched a smoke bomb attack on a Dutch royal wedding procession.[7] Faithful to their anarchist philosophy, the Dutch Provos self-destructed in 1967 when some of their members became involved in council elections and they realized they were being sucked into a liberal political establishment.

Situationist theory has been invoked as the cultural ancestor of the explosive Punk movement, most memorably in *Lipstick Traces* (1989) by Greil Marcus. His genealogy is strengthened by the likelihood that some of the groups, for instance The Clash and Adam and the Ants, were exposed in art schools to cultural traditions of dissent through Dadaism; and while this obviously overlooks the English working-class origins of Punk, there is no doubt that the movement enacted key ideas of Situationism. The designer-style, superstar groups that Punk spat on were prime examples of the spectacle but, always, the explosive energy and speed of punk was more than a musical phenomenon. Insurrectional Punk assaulted the alienated life that lay behind the society of the spectacle, and the powerlessness of the proletariat damningly united the unemployed, the low-waged, the office worker and the 'professional' into a shared well of negation and isola-tion: the proletarianization of the world, as Debord labelled it. *Lipstick Traces* grapples with the difficulty of aligning cultural moments across time, linking Johnny Rotten with a Guy Debord whom the singer had never heard of, but Greil Marcus seizes the fecundity that just such a skewed approach offers and, in doing so, ushers both movements into the anar-chist tradition.[8]

In a quite different arena, the Situationist idea of 'psychogeography' was ahead of its time in seeking to challenge and reconfigure individuals' psychological relationships with their urban environment. *Détournement* was to be enacted in games and pranks that would be played out on urban sites, and one of the groups that founded the Situationist International published a 'Plan for Improving the Rationality of the City of Paris' in 1955 that called for opening public gardens at night and building escalators to rooftops so as to create aerial pavements. Another Situationist, Ivan Chtcheglov, enthused over the liberating power of buildings that would engage with and release emotions in the citizens of the streets, a psychic, fantasy architecture where the design of different rooms and constructs would connect with a range of feelings being trivialized and reified by an excess of material satisfaction. The Situationist's interrogation of urban space looked forward to contemporary anarchist-inspired movements like Critical Mass and Reclaim the Streets, which strive to reclaim overregulated public spaces. Critical Mass has spread around the world from its 1992 origins in the US, and what started life as a local attempt to oppose car junkies and SUVs in the Bay Area has grown to embody one of the central strategies of the anti-capitalist movement: the physicist's notion of critical mass becoming a political metaphor for the possibility of leaderless, mass action precipitating a direct action dynamic of explosive social power. In a similar jagged trajectory, Reclaim the Streets sprang to life in London in the early 1990s before spreading across Europe, Australia and the Americas, and its anarchist heritage was highlighted during the 1997 general election in Britain by fusing The Sex Pistols, direct action and the futility of voting under the banner 'Never Mind the Ballots, Reclaim the Streets'. Jeff Ferrell, in the upbeat *Tearing Down the Streets Adventures in Urban Anarchy*,[9] situates these and other forms of decentralized, leaderless activities, like skateboarding, BASE jumping (parachuting from Buildings, Antennas, Spans and Earth), hiphop graffiti writing, outlawed microradio broadcasting, walking itself, to the same broad anarchist impulse to subvert the controlled hierarchies expressed through sanitized forms of urban power.

The anarchist-inspired activities described by Ferrell offer alternative experiences of public, cultural spaces and oppose the gentrification of urban spaces that is part of the process of class control. In the name of public safety a Kafkaesque proliferation of urban surveillance systems disguises the need to address the causes of social crimes. Similarly, notions of 'zero tolerance' and 'quality of life' crimes hide their class nature behind spurious but appealing ideas of civility and urban contentment.

The Politics of Desire

Situationism also touched on sexuality, a subject that receives more attention in anarchist thought than in traditional communist or socialist writing. In 1967 Raoul Vaneigem, a key figure in Situationist International, published *The Revolution of Everyday Life*, a book that provided many a slogan daubed on the walls of Paris in 1968, including the lengthiest of all:

THOSE WHO SPEAK OF REVOLUTION AND CLASS STRUGGLE WITH EXPLICIT REFERENCES TO EVERYDAY LIFE, WITHOUT UNDERSTANDING THE SUBVERSIVENESS OF LOVE AND WHAT'S POSITIVE IN THE REFUSAL OF CONSTRAINTS, THEY HAVE A CADAVER IN THEIR MOUTHS.

The Blakean echo of the sentiment points to anarchism's conviction that the relationship between sexual and political freedom is an important one, that internalized structures of repression are linked with the willingness of some people to accept political control to the point of craving authority. In this respect, and not for the first time, anarchists look to the history of the communist government in Russia after 1917 as an indication of what can happen to a revolutionary movement that lacks a libertarian soul. In the tumultuous early months of Bolshevik rule, reactionary legislation affecting sex and gender issues was swept away by new marriage decrees.

Divorce was made easy, full legal rights were accorded to marriage-less families, and the legalization of abortion and homosexuality was to follow. As political authoritarianism took root, however, and in a process paralleling the collapse of Russia's cultural revolution in other areas of life, the radical legislation was revoked and official attitudes towards sexuality in the USSR became not hugely different from those existing in western European states.

Stirner's 'wheels in the head' and Blake's 'mind-forg'd manacles' are as difficult to escape from as material constraints, but libertarian socialists look to elements of Wilhelm Reich's social psychology, allied to Blake's own anarchist spirit of revolt, as a means of release. Reich provides an escape route from certain reactionary implications of classical psychoanalysis, whereby instinctual and undisciplined sexuality has to be necessarily sublimated in order for civilization to exist, and the tenor of the anarchist's counter-claim is given rich expression in Blake's poetry. Blake's metaphysical dialectic, in poems like *The Marriage of Heaven and Hell*, builds on contraries ('The tygers of wrath are wiser than the horses of instruction . . . Improvement makes strait roads; but the crooked roads without Improvement are roads of Genius . . . The cistern contains: the fountain overflows'), asserting that 'Energy is Eternal Delight' and that:

> Those who restrain desire, do so because theirs is weak enough to
> be restrained; and the restrainer or reason usurps its place &
> governs the unwilling: And being restrain'd, it by degrees
> becomes passive, till it is only the shadow of desire.[10]

In giving voice to the role of culture in the creation of sexual repression, Blake delineates a bond between aggression and forms of repression ('For war is energy Enslav'd'[11]) that would later be explored by Reich in the context of twentieth-century European Fascism. Reich's *The Mass Psychology of Fascism* was written during World War II, and in it he quotes from a newspaper article he read in *The New York Times* as an example of murderous militarism:

> The German Afrika Corps defeated the Eighth Army because it had speed, anger, vitality and toughness. As soldiers in the traditional sense, the Germans are punk, absolutely punk . . . The German commanders are scientists, who are continually experimenting with and improving the hard, mathematical formula of killing . . . War is pure physics to them . . . The German soldier is trained with a psychology of the daredevil track rider.[12]

Reich, in seeking to understand how a person becomes such a mechanical and sadistic killer, sees humanity as dichotomized into an animal part, biologically driven to seek sexual gratification, food, sharing a kinship with nature, and another part that seeks to deny the animal level and progress instead through mechanical structures of organization and thought. Machines open the way to a tremendous expansion of 'man's biologic organizations', but this process has developed into a 'machine civilization' that invites the creation of rigid hierarchies and encourages a mechanistic view of human biology. In this way, the brain becomes the commander-in-chief of the body's organs and a statist pedagogy takes hold:

> Infants have to drink a precise quantity of milk at fixed intervals and have to sleep a precise number of hours. Their diet has to have exactly x ounces of fat, y ounces of protein and z pounces of carbohydrates . . . Children have to study x hours of mathematics, y hours of chemistry, z hours of zoology, all exactly the same, and all of them have to acquire the same amount of wisdom. Superior intelligence is equal to one hundred points, average intelligence to eighty points, stupidity to forty points.[13]

This mechanistic process goes hand in hand with economic development, and people are taught to armour themselves against the natural and spontaneous until 'they are filled with mortal fear of the living and the free'. Reich goes on to relate this to the hierarchical order of the state, a fear of responsibility and 'an intense longing for a führer and craving for authority'.

Reich himself was never an anarchist, but the early expression of his theories about human sexuality, informed as they are by Marxism and the realization that ideology can be a material force, have been adopted by anarchism as a way of understanding why people do not reject forms of authority that so obviously impair their capacity for joyful existence. It is easy to ridicule Reich's notion of 'orgastic potency' by bluntly reducing it to the belief that sexual energy and its release through orgasm is the root cause of a person's health, or lack of it, and in later years Reich certainly invited ridicule in some of the ways he expressed his ideas. Reich's theory, though, needs to be seen in the context of the ideas developed in his *Character Analysis* and the way in which its account of the id differs from Freud's. For Reich, the human makeup has three components which, in terms of depth, begin at root level in a spontaneous capacity to enjoy work and social relations. This natural capacity is unnecessarily repressed by culture and hence the unconscious which is the unhealthy mix pretty much as Freud describes it. This leads to a third level, the social mask of inauthenticity, that Reich calls the 'character' and which is equivalent to the Freudian ego except that Reich saw the ego as unhealthy. Instead of being a necessary defence against what Freud called the 'cauldron' of the id, the ego for Reich was an unpleasant and unhealthy response to the unconscious. The aim of therapy was the removal of character and the release of 'orgastic potency', and to do this involved revealing the particular means whereby an individual encased his psychic energy, i.e., his character. Relinquishing accounts of dreams, slips of the tongue, jokes, Reich looked to the manner of a person's speech more than the actual verbal content, realizing that *how* a person uses language is more revealing than what is actually said.

As well as being open to many of the charges that it has become fashionable to direct at Freud, any adoption of some of Reich's ideas needs to carry further qualification on account of their simplicity and *naïveté*. But while the utopian and Rousseauesque side to Reich is always in danger of slipping into a psychoanalytic version of primitivism, anarchism appreciates what is valuable about his attempt to fuse Marx and Freud and help dismantle one of the dominant paradigms of our culture. Reich related his theories to the repressive nature of society and realized that liberation depended not so much on the psychiatrist's couch as on an alteration in social and sexual relations that itself depended on political change. A member of the Austrian Communist Party, he set up party sex clinics in the late 1920s in the Vienna area, but they were closed down because Party apparatchiks regarded them as distractions from the main cause. They were deaf to his argument that the repressive ideology of capitalism became internalized in people and that, in line with Marxist material philosophy, an individual's repression became part of his or her nature. For Reich, the Russian Revolution of 1917 went sour because it failed to challenge patriarchal sexuality and the family, which meant that people remained submissive and repressed. His promotion of adolescent sexuality and masturbation as healthy activities help explain his expulsion from the Communist Party in the early 1930s, and Reich would eventually abandon Marxism and politics altogether. Therapy became physical, replacing a 'talking cure' by programmes designed to adjust the physiological reality of the libido, leading to his 'discovery' of a life force, Orgone energy, measurable with an Orgone Energy Field Meter. He moved to the USA in 1939, after his ideas received short change in Oslo, where he had been developing them, and he ended up almost paranoid, dying in the prison in which he had been incarcerated after a ridiculous dispute over his Accumulator (a masturbating machine).

Despite the fact that Freud is now being reinterpreted as an imaginative, metaphysical storyteller, the reactionary reading of his work still holds sway. This posits humans as fundamentally licentious and amoral, necessitating repressive control in order to keep at bay the irrational impulses that lurk threateningly in the mind. In this context Reich remains important because he brought a radical and political interpretation to Freud, pointing forward to the possibilities of a humane and happy life for humanity, one that speaks of celebrating the erotic rather than containing it.

It might seem that the acceptance of progressively more liberal attitudes to sexuality and the abandonment of many sexual taboos, at least in some parts of the world, reveals an inherent inadequacy in relating sexual repression to political control. This, however, rests on a limited notion of sexual liberation that conveniently brackets off the alienating world of work and class that informs sexual relations. It also underestimates the continuing role of patriarchy and the family in creating psychic structures of conformity, and ignores consumer capitalism's creative ability to commodify and thereby diminish the progressive value of modern attitudes to sexual behaviour. In one sense – strictly contained within geographically and culturally defined regions – there has been a sexual revolution, but it has been accompanied by new ways of alienating and reifying sexuality. Just as modern capitalism has absorbed, learnt to accommodate and recuperate from working-class political demands, so too is it learning to come to terms – but in its own terms – with gay and lesbian life, teenage sexuality and other aspects of more liberated attitudes towards sexuality. Ultimately, anarchism is not trying to suggest that contesting issues of sexuality can ever be a substitute or replacement for political struggle, that the perfect orgasm leads to better class war, but what anarchists insist on is the compound and complex consequences of class relations and the fact that issues of sexuality and desire are intimately bound up with the exercise of political power and questions of authority and obedience. Just such a medley of ideas informs Elio Petri's 1971 film,

The Working Class Goes to Heaven, about a steelworker, Ludovico Massa. The effects of Massa's baleful routine of alienated labour is etched on his fatigued face, shown in close-up at the start of the film, and his mechanical sexual life. Before a work accident severs his finger, the Stakhanovite steelworker whose nickname is 'Lulu the tool', both at work and in bed at home, embodies Reich's notion, developed in *The Function of the Orgasm*, that man not only believes he is a machine but 'does actually function automatically, mechanistically and mechanically'.[14]

Such issues, and the experiences that give rise to them, are rarely addressed in traditional left-wing thought, even though they touch on matters of felt concern to most people, whatever their level of political consciousness. They are explored by non-anarchist artists in works of literature, like Shakespeare in *Measure for Measure* in 1604, probing topics in a manner that cuts across the usual spectrum of political art and aesthetics. Shakespeare's play dissects the dialectic of sexuality as a repressive city governor, Angelo, whose first words are 'Always obedient . . .', finds himself tortured with desire for Isabella, a young woman about to become a nun, when she comes to plead for the life of her brother, whom Angelo has sentenced to death for a sexual transgression. An unsentimental compassion accrues to Angelo as his profound lack of happiness is rawly exposed and he comes to sense his own forfeiture of joy to what he calls 'the manacles of the all-binding law'. The drama's concern with law and desire successfully avoids a retreat to the conservatism that Freud would later give expression to in *Civilization and its Discontents*, with the play's depth proving too much for a literary genre that usually concludes with an uncomplicated celebration of marriage and the social order. The sexual act between the condemned man and his lover emerges as the only unblemished relationship in the story, and Lucio, the character who rejects sexual ethics, is the one person who can win over the audience's sympathy and delight.

Measure for Measure's subversive tensions and ambiguities, which largely account for its status as one of Shakespeare's 'problem plays', are especially pronounced because they are *not* emanating from a avowedly libertarian position. When self-consciously anarchist art focuses on sexuality, a film like Claude Faraldo's *Bof* (1971) succeeds in seditiously celebrating liberation by way of an insouciant disruption of sexual conformity. The film, made four years after Faraldo gave up his work as a delivery man, begins with the soul-destroying boredom of just such a job. The young delivery man, working for a wine firm in Paris, is lucky enough to catch the eye of a young woman, Germaine, in a shop window. They set up home, and then the man's father, a person well qualified to rebel against an existence of alienating work ('Twenty-five years, minus holidays, tell me how many times I clocked in?'), throws in his job and moves in with them. Germaine agrees to her father-in-law's suggestion that they make love, and a happy household takes shape around the three of them. The young man also gives up his job and they head for the south of France together. *Bof* has been criticized on the grounds that it offers little more than an immature escapism,[15] but this misses the spirit of the anarchist *Zeitgeist*, expressed in the film's title and its joyful ideas of sexual revelry, and the way in which it contributes to the provocative aesthetic. The film's eulogizing of sensual license, far from being adolescent or sexist, is more a metaphor for why rebellion is worthwhile and necessary than a discourse on alternatives to repressive family structures. The dialogue is deliberately simple, to the point of banality, because Faraldo is not concerned with developing an argument as such but infusing the narrative with a mood of subversion by *not* raising the kind of concerns that conventional cinema would bring to such a story. *Bof* succeeds by cherishing what the bohemianism of its characters represents, and the idyllic long-shot of their rural stroll that ends the film offers a filmic and rhetorical counter to the opening images of the alienated workplace. The sexual congresses in *Bof* signify the beginning of a group breakout from class-based society in a way that is the direct opposite of those in Alfonso Cuaron's *Y Tu Mama Tambien* (2001). In Cuaron's film the liberating and egalitarian sexual antics of Tenoch and Julio come to signify a closure, given that they are on the cusp of taking up their adult positioning within the class hierarchy of contemporary Mexican society.

The exultation of desire as an anti-hierarchical force, so evident in an anarchist film like *Bof* as well as the non-anarchist *Y Tu Mama Tambien*, has a cinematic genealogy going back to Surrealism and Luis Buñuel's *L'Age d'or* (1930). The film celebrates revolt, in a Blake-like opposition of reason and desire, by having a statist occasion – peopled by 'soldiers, priests, monks, nuns, policemen and silkhatted civilians'[16] – ruptured by a couple's vigorous lovemaking, which comes to a premature end when the woman is pulled away by the shocked upholders of religion and the state. Elsewhere, the struggle takes place within the individual's psyche, as in the scene when the enraged hero flings a fir-tree, followed by a plough, a giraffe, an archbishop and bunches of feathers out of a window, representing, according to one interpretation, family, work, honour, religion and material comforts.[17] Buñuel's anti-clericalism and anti-authoritarianism were just as potent a force decades later when he came to make *Viridiana* (1961). The film's eponymous character is about to become a nun, and, like Shakespeare's Isabella, there is a hint of repressed sensuality in her chilly Christianity – a wooden cross, nails and a crown of thorns turning up in her luggage when she travels to the house of her uncle before taking her vows. Like Isabella, she attracts the lascivious attention of a man, her uncle, who consequently suffers pangs of guilt and hangs himself. This precipitates the film's ascent into delicious blasphemy, as the perturbed young woman gathers a group of grotesque beggars and invites them into the house in a confused attempt at redemption. The beggars enjoy to the full the opportunity presented and the orgy that follows climaxes in a Rabelaisian inversion of Leonardo's *Last Supper* and the molestation of Viridiana. As well as being Buñuel's triumphant riposte to Franco and Catholicism – offering a cinematic middle digit to the Spanish dictator's invitation to return from exile in Mexico and make a film of his own choice – *Viridiana* delights in showing that liberation will not come from above, and least of all from ascetic, life-denying moralities.

Anarchism and Surrealism are not synonymous, but as cultural states of minds, as *spirit*, there are family resemblances. They share a provocative intent to discredit common suppositions about our possibilities for being, claiming that our consciousness is incomplete if, confusing how things are with how they could be, desire is distrusted and repressed. The capacity to change reality is part of being, and Marxist ontology is given a Surrealist twist: 'Man proposes and disposes. It is simply up to him to belong entirely to himself, that is, to maintain in a state of anarchy the band of his desires which will each day become more formidable.'[18] Before the Holocaust proved them prophets, Surrealists and anarchist artists like Blake, Shelley and Wilde saw what could be hidden and repressed in the guise of ratio-nality, and this helps explain why the spirit of revolt that lies at the heart of Surrealism is equally important to cultural anarchism. Blasphemy, revolt and disorder – in a move that distances them completely from the unfet-tered license of unreason – are valued positively because of what they negate. André Breton, like many Surrealists, came to realize that scaring bourgeois sensibilities could slide into merely titillating them, and his awareness of this possibility lay behind his estrangement from Salvador Dalí. Breton knew that art was not a shortcut to social revolution, and he turned to communism in the hope of building a bridge between the libera-tion of the individual's mind and the larger transformation of society. He understood Marx's position that truth is not an independent entity but constitutive with knowledge, and his unhappy experience with a Communist Party incapable of accommodating libertarianism did not prevent him from trying to forge a praxis that allied Surrealism with direct action. Surrealism's first political stand was against France's colonial war in Morocco, and politically aware Surrealists joined picket lines and fought against Franco in the Spanish Civil War.

An Anarchist Aesthetic?

Films like *Bof* and a movement like Surrealism raise the bothersome question as to whether there is, or could be, an anarchist aesthetic. Anarchism has been seen as taking aesthetic shape in the form of modernism, building on features of modernism that share an affinity with aspects of cultural anarchism, in particular the espousal of art as an anti-official form of freedom and autonomy and the awareness of the limitations of rationalism. Modernism, however, belongs to a particular moment in history and an anarchist aesthetic cannot equate itself with such a moment without limiting its validity. Aspects of Surrealism, after all, have been expropriated by the advertising industry, and any putative anarchist aesthetic cannot fail to acknowledge acts of incorporation like this. What may be at stake is the value of any form of cultural anarchism that does not emerge from, or accompany, a politically focused movement of the libertarian left. There is also the fact that where cultural anarchism does overlap with particular aspects of modernism, it is usually only the individualistic strain of anarchism that comes to the fore. Consequently, and none too surprisingly, the result is likely to lead to a mere politics of style, the kind of postmodern, lifestyle anarchism that celebrates fragmentation, plurality and difference while conveniently putting to one side questions of class exploitation.

The course of just such a trajectory can be traced in the US, going back to the first two decades of the 20th century, when modernism was suffused with anarchist principles. The artist and art teacher Robert Henri read Bakunin and Wilde, attended lectures by Emma Goldman, and sought to politicize art by encouraging artistic individuality in the belief that this would engender an engagement with the material world of social struggle. The values of American Establishment art were attacked as authoritarian, imposing bourgeois culture, whereas the freedom of expression that was vital to the artist was seen as part of the same freedom that every individual had a right to. Among American anarchist artists like Henri there was a clearheaded recognition that the attainment of such a freedom was incompatible with free market economics and the class system, and they tried to forge a movement that would fuse artistic liberation with revolutionary politics. *Anarchist Modernism*, a study of the impact of libertarianism on the American avant-garde, charts in detail the impact of anarchism on artists like Man Ray, Rockwell Kent and Robert Minor and seeks to account for the collapse of the current of cultural anarchism to which they contributed.[19] The failure was clearly linked to the broader collapse of political anarchism in the United States, aided by concerted government repression, and the haemorrhaging of political support for anarchism caused by the Bolshevik revolution in Russia in 1917. The fate of the cartoonist Robert Minor, an avowed anarchist who was dismissed from the *New York Evening Post* in 1915 because of his anti-war cartoons and for contributing to *Mother Earth*, edited by Emma Goldman and Alexander Berkman, sums up the sorry decline and fall. Minor visited World War I's French front lines and returned to produce some searingly effective cartoons for a New York socialist newspaper and for *Golos Truda*, a weekly paper for the 10,000-strong anarchist Union of Russian Workers of the United States and Canada. One of his more famous cartoons, depicting a colossal, blood-soaked and sword-wielding executioner wading through a swamp of blood and body parts, entitled 'Civilization', appeared in both newspapers. Minor left the USA for Petrograd in April 1918, saw for himself the Bolshevik repression of Russian anarchists and returned to the States at the end of the year to broadcast what was happening. Attacked and cajoled by socialists who could not admit that the Russian revolution was in danger from the authoritarian Bolshevik party, Minor succumbed to the argument that criticism of the Bolsheviks provided ammunition for anti-communist propaganda. He repented and wrote an article entitled 'I Change My Mind a Little' before joining the Communist Party and eventually aban-doning his art 'because Lenin never drew cartoons but devoted his full time to politics'.[20] The American government's repression of anarchist organizations and the conflict of loyalties presented by the Revolution in Russia undoubtedly played a large part in the demise of anarchist art in the US, but another important factor was the disproportionate influence of the tradition of individualist anarchism in that country. An artist like Man Ray was more influenced by the politically dubious individualism of European Vorticist art than communist anarchism. *The Egoist* journal, one of the voices of the Vorticist movement, was named after Stirner's *The Ego and Its Own* and attracted Ezra Pound and Wyndham Lewis, artists who may have responded warmly to the extreme individualism of Stirner and Nietzsche but not in a way that contributes much to anarchism.[21]

A crude argument against the value of anarchist art is that revolutionary activity requires disciplined organization, and that libertarian chatter about psychic structures of restraint and obedience are of little import when confronting the challenge of removing the class system. Just such an argument was levelled at artists like Robert Minor, and a standard anarchist rejoinder is that while cultural forms of rebellion do not seek to replace political and social struggle they do make an important contribution to the task of raising consciousness and exposing fault lines in systems of control and exploitation. While this may be true, it contributes little to the question of whether there can be something called an anarchist aesthetic. Attempts to understand certain forms of art as being intrinsically more anarchist than others are not convincing. The anarchist American painter Walter Pach, for instance, fruitlessly argued that by abandoning mimesis in favour of abstraction, Cubism was championing a collectivist spirit and aiding revolt.[22] This is completely at odds with an earlier anarchist, Proudhon, who regarded Realism as the epitome of radical art, praising the work of Gustave Courbet in this regard and receiving the support of Courbet for just such an equivalence of form with political progressiveness.

In the end, an anarchist aesthetic can only exist as part of a broader cultural and political movement for radical change along non-hierarchical, libertarian principles. Art is a derivative of life, and anarchism is about living a certain kind of life, the type of existence that Emma Goldman was referring to when she spoke of only wanting a revolution she could dance to. Art that engages with the kind of political, cultural and personal change relevant to such an end has a claim on the notion of anarchist aesthetics. Such an anti-essentialist and non-prescriptive definition is necessarily a loose one, but it has the virtue of being compatible with a whole gamut of art forms, from Shelley's paean to the anarchist imagination in *A Defence of Poetry* to works of fiction like Ursula Le Guin's *The Dispossessed*, as well as, perhaps, more recent agitational, anti-art currents like neoism, with its faint echoes of Dadaism. So catholic a formalization might also just about include, without seriously embracing, the kind of pranks that with the help of a generous disposition could be viewed as forms of American *détourne-ment*. Occupying the margins of this iconoclasm is the likes of Reverend Ivan Stang's Church of the SubGenius. Stang, alias J. R. 'Bob' Dobbs, paro-dying the pipe-smoking salesman of post-WWII consumer America, who offers a spoof salvation from the predicted apocalypse (originally set for 5 July 1988 but revised in the light of what didn't happen) by way of an escape from earth with the assistance of alien beings. With an ironic gospel of un-American values, the Church of the SubGenius has spread its message in print, film and happenings.[23]

Chic Subversions

There are difficulties with the looseness of the above notion of an anar-chist aesthetic because it can be stretched to a point where its meaningful relevance to anarchism never leaves the armchair of the libertarian theorist. What, after all, do pranks like the Reverend Ivan

Stang's Church of the SubGenius amount to? In theory they sound fine, as argued in the introduction to a book, *Pranks*, that documents the work of a variety of outrageous artists and personalities:

> Calling into question inherently dubious concepts such as 'reality', 'trust', 'obedience', and 'the social contract', pranks occasionally succeed in implanting a profound and lasting distrust of all social conventions and institutions.[24]

Perhaps, 'occasionally', they do, but couldn't the same be said about Ridley Scott movies, Monty Python sketches and a whole lot more? Advanced capitalism, mercifully assuming it has reached its advanced stage, is not only well able to accommodate 'subversive' pranks but may even depend on them as a creative source for tapping into new, previously unexploited areas of social and cultural life. Pranks combine good fun with politics when they occur in situations where the uncompromising point of the humour is made explicit, and the Reverend Ivan Stang counts for little when put alongside antics like those of the Reverend Billy and The Church of Stop Shopping. Performing as part of a group, the Reverend Billy has preached not-so-divine truths about the coffee industry to congregations of Starbucks outlets in New York.[25] Or there is Noël Godin's siege machine, a military catapult the size of a house and surprisingly accurate within a range of 35 metres. When employed in an anti-capitalist demonstration it serves a wonderful purpose – it was to be used outside the courtroom where José Bové was on trial for dismantling a McDonald's restaurant and leaving the parts outside the local town hall, until it was realized that its accuracy against members of the judiciary would most likely increase Bové's sentence – but can the same be said of Godin's 'flanning' of public figures like Bill Gates? Landing a cream pie on the face of the famous may be jolly good fun in its deflation of pompous egos, but, again, so what? A lot of what loosely passes for being anarchic in its nature, especially in a postmodernist idiom, is practised by people who in five years' time may well be earnestly working for the type of organizations they were supposedly intent on subverting. This is certainly not the case with Noël Godin, a dedicated anarchist from the days of May 1968, but it is not cynical to think that some of the young hacktivists of today will be the Microsoft executives of tomorrow. For an anarchist like Murray Bookchin, antics like those of the Church of the SubGenius are the infantile distractions of ego-centered yuppies – and he is probably right. Even if he is not right, such practices of subversion have a habit, however anti-hierarchical, of being incorporated into a sophisticated and highly creative cultural order capable of handling contradictions and in the process making them 'insouciant, but deliciously safe'.[26]

When used in certain cultural and artistic contexts, the concept of anarchism can be too slippery and catholic for its own good. Sharing the role of some forms of postmodernism in this respect, it becomes part of a fairly hollow discourse that too glibly assumes rationality and humanism are being subversively deconstructed as part of a radical assault on the capitalist order. In the case of a thinker like Nietzsche, there is a rich complexity to his onslaught on rationalism and humanism, a complexity that resists attempts to explore it in trifling ways; but when postmodernism slips into sweeping observations about 'post-industrial' reality, the resulting generalizations have a ring of shallowness despite their coolness. In an issue of *Anarchist Studies* devoted to science fiction, for example, the likes of postmodernists such as Jean Baudrillard and Jean-François Lyotard are declared

> anarchists because the critiques they develop constitute, in part, a massive theoretical challenge to the very existence of capital and the state . . . Postmodern anarchism challenges an entire psychology and an entire semiotic structure which underwrite the dominant system of political economy.[27]

The possibility that this just might be a little too heady and rarefied to amount to much becomes more pronounced when the claims being made about a certain kind of science fiction are assessed. Particular works of science fiction are seen to constitute a revolutionary project because of their prescient awareness of the unstable nature of language. Building on the postmodernist platitude that separates the signifier from the signified, and making language the source of its own analysis, science fiction of a certain kind becomes a metaphor for revolutionary struggle of an anarchist kind:

> In science fiction, a rocket leaves the earth, rises up and up, higher and higher: at the initial stages, gravity asserts itself on all within. But then, once acceleration has pushed the vehicle past the seven miles per second escape velocity, then acceleration may cease: with cessation comes the release of the gravitic effect, which is replaced by the weightless state, free-fall, in which all prior gravitic organizations become malleable, trivial, a mere cross section of the complex locus of current objective trajectories within the ship's confines. Space is that topos not organised by up and down, day or night. Light sources do not play over a gradient transition of hues – there is no atmosphere to refract. Worlds, because they are so far away, can not constrain all effort into difficult ascents, easy descents, and equiposed horizontals . . . then a conceptual freedom is broached that the earth-bound consciousness has seldom been able to maintain for any length of time.[28]

This may sound great – an anarchist aesthetic indeed – but is it any more than verbal hype? In fact, when 'worlds' is replaced by 'words' in the last sentence, the quotation becomes a charming trope for postmodernist ambitions, but not a great deal more than this. The cyberpunk fiction of William Gibson and Bruce Sterling, for example, has been praised for its postmodern anarchism because of the way human subjectivity is radically reconfigured in a way that challenges conventional ideas of rationality and space. By wiring up the 'mind' of machine technologies with human consciousness, the cyborg world that emerges is seen to herald a seditious assault on bourgeois semiotics, one that sketches a new kind of insurrectionary micro-politics. In Bruce Sterling's *Holy Fire*, for instance, the government at the end of the twenty-first century takes the form of a powerful medical–industrial complex that is opposed by a group of avant-garde Situationist-leaning rebels ('Beneath the beach – The Pavement',[29] runs the graffiti in a 'psychogeographic' part of town favoured by their Guy Debord-like theoretician). The ruling class of 'posthuman' gerontocrats govern a world that is close to achieving biological immortality, but the mere prolongation of longevity is not enough for a group of bohemian dissidents who realize that they are the first of the new generation that could live for over a millennium. Rejecting a risk-free world of terminal boredom, they challenge the status quo by seeking the 'holy fire'– the existential dimension that makes life worth living – and using their technological skills to introduce a cognitive enhancement to their near-cyborg destiny. In William Gibson's *Idoru*, like *Holy Fire* published in 1996, a legendary group of disaffected netusers are credited with having created Hak Nam ('City of Darkness') by hacking into the net, deleting its commercial content and authoritarian structures and turning what is left into what is also called the Walled City:

> the people who founded Hak Nam were angry, because the net had been very free, you could do what you wanted, but then the governments and the companies, they had different ideas of what you could, what you couldn't do. So these people, they found a way to unravel something. A little place, a piece, like a cloth. They made something like a killfile of *everything*, everything they didn't like, and they turned that inside out . . . They went there to get away from the laws. To have no laws, like when the net was new.[30]

Cyberpunk is partly characterized by neat, throw-away concepts like the Walled City, but such ideas hardly constitute an attempt to dismantle bourgeois forms of reality, especially when they occur within novels like *Idoru* that are utterly conventional in their narrative form. *Holy Fire*, with its alluring descriptions and thought-provoking moments, is fun to read even though its ending is so well-balanced and reasonable as to be almost cheesy, but the claim being made for its anarchist intent seems as inane as the conclusion that one critic arrives at: 'The barricades of the next revolution will be raised in post-Cartesian virtual space, and this revolution will be carried out by cyborgs who reject an outmoded, bourgeois rational subjectivity. If we are not prepared for this revolution, we risk being delegated to the dustbin of history.'[31] The absurdity is not a reflection on the intrinsic merits of the fiction of Gibson or Sterling, but arises from the postmodernist flimflam with which such writing is invested.

Some subversions remain chic because at a very basic level hierarchical divisions are not synonymous with the class structuring of society. To realize this, however, is not to retreat to narrow-minded pontifications based on a set of purist principles that reduces everything to class struggle. Far from it, because anarchists are acutely aware of the fact that the existence of hierarchies broadens the nature of what it means to radically challenge capitalism. Hierarchies are divisions of rank arising from the distribution of power and wealth, while exploitation is the appropriation of the economic surplus produced by working people, and class is a common factor that links the two. They overlap in varied ways, conspicuously so in the way women are dominated in relation to the production of work and the structure of the family. Sometimes, the question of which came first is like the chicken and egg configuration. It is possible, as Bookchin argues, that class divisions have a source in primitive hierarchies and that the rise of chiefs in early communities created an incipient hierarchy that evolved over time and in conjunction with social and economic forces, principally the production of surplus production and wars of conquest, into the beginnings of class structure.

What works against a simple equation of class exploitation with hierarchy is the possibility of hierarchies surviving the removal of class divisions, something borne out in the history of Russian and Cuban communism. Such hierarchies become institutionalized systems of domination, despite the removal of class divisions, although the nature of the privileges enjoyed by those occupying a dominating position need not be economic in their nature. The hierarchies that developed in Soviet society brought undoubted material advantages to elite individuals and groups, but such gains were not the *raison d'être* of their existence. In the *Republic*, Plato does not envisage the guardians enjoying a life of material luxury, while in the fiction of Le Guin's *The Dispossessed* the nascent hierarchy is emerging from the bureaucracy and the social authority of individuals within it. In the real world, the oppression of women is bound up with hierarchy in a way that transcends traditional class divisions, and direct action itself is capable of creating an incipient hierarchy between those who take on leading roles and those who participate in less theatrical ways. An example that has been pointed to was the protest against the building of a road bypass near Newbury, England, in the mid-1990s,[32] when the kudos that accrued to the activists squatting 30 feet up in trees led to an over-emphasis on their action at the expense of supporters, literally on the ground. This made the task of the roadbuilders a relatively straightforward one of hiring their own tree-climbers and mounting a successful early morning raid on the protestors. Consequently, a situation with the potential for a formidable mass protest was broken down by targeting one group of activists who had become identified as the force of the direct action. Such a mistake was not made at Seattle in 1999 or at the anti-capitalist protests since then, where no one group emerges, or wants to emerge, as the sole face of the action.

CHAPTER SIX

The Anarchist Tension

Marx did not attempt a clinical analysis of a post-capitalist world; nor did he try to offer a programme for life under communism. The future was an open book, and by his own philosophy – an ontology of becoming – this was necessarily so, a state of infinite possibilities and endless possible states of self-fulfilment. Given that everything is always in a state of becoming it is not, in the sense that an anarchism allied to Marx allows for, about thinking the unthinkable or demanding the impossible. People's being cannot be fulfilled until alienation and class exploitation is overcome, and what might then unfold is best left to the imagination. This is what Marx does, more than once, in his evocative imagining of the post-capitalist individual accommodating labour time within a broader dimension of work and play. Life's possibilities go well beyond the world of work and in a liberated world people would not be pressed into building their lives around their work. The same flexible approach to the future characterizes the anti-capitalist movement in that it is not committing itself to a specific alternative system that must be implemented in order to replace existing social relations. The focus is on the here and now, the in-your-face greed and violence of capitalism that can no longer hide itself behind the ideology of the Cold War. It was the immediate context of the post-Cold War world, the 1990s, that fostered the new anti-capitalist movement. It was a time which saw the erasure of old political positions – the Cold War warrior, or the apologist for the USSR, or the disaffected liberal sitting on the fence – and the emergence of a pan-anti-capitalist movement that focused on the global nature of the dominant economic system.

Anarchist thought and action has always been worldwide, but, being the continent that first saw the death of feudalism and the rise of capitalism, it was post-French Revolution Europe that saw the clear emergence of the modern anarcho-communist tradition. The coming of the millennium has confirmed the force of globalized capitalism, and what is indeed likely to be a weakening of the nation state, ushering in a new north–south battleground that goes beyond national boundaries. The anti-capitalist movement, in its libertarian spirit and commitment to direct action, its decentralized organizations, its organisms, and its vision of a future not governed by the profit motive or the dictates of doctrinaire left-wing groups, is part of this battle and the battle for anarchism.

The enemy is no longer seen solely in terms of this or that particular state but also in terms of broader organizations like the IMF and the World Bank, executive bodies that administer and push forward modern capitalism on a planned, globalized basis. Such bodies have partly usurped the role of national states, taken on many of their powers and adopted the same ideological armour, something that becomes readily apparent when listening to their *déjà vu* defence of globalization. Allow a small sector of the population to increase their wealth, it is argued, and this leads to a trickle-down effect that eventually benefits everyone because of the greater economic growth. Conservative free-marketeers and their politicians on national stages have always relied on this argument when seeking to dress their party's ideology in something reasonable and respectable, only now it is presented as a global argument for the whole world. Moreover, just as opposition to the injustices and inequalities of the free market took moderate and revolutionary forms within nation states, so too is opposition to globalization. Reformers think that a dialogue with the World Bank and the IMF is possible and that a deeply flawed system can be made more accountable and democratic. This is liberal democracy, the Third Way, an invitation to the cartel of capitalists to make a few concessions and adjustments and preserve the status quo. Radical opposition to globalization challenges globalization with localization and seeks to dismantle the capitalist architecture. This does not mean the end of long-distance trade altogether, but the principle of producing locally in the first instance, and trading long distance for what is not available locally, runs counter to the ideological and economic thrust of free-market globalization. Instead of ruthless competition for market shares and the search for lower costs, which translates into pitifully low wages and child labour in Third World sweatshops, localization prioritizes local production and small producers. Bananas, tea, coffee and the like still need to be imported in Europe, for example, but localization also throws up interesting possibilities (allotments in Birmingham, England, are now the biggest source of coriander in Europe), not least by questioning the purpose served by an economy. Free-market globalization is premised on the principle that it is good to compete internationally and seek out lower costs, whereas localization asserts the primacy of meeting people's fundamental needs without global competition.

Anarchists are not Luddites and, far from being blind to the ongoing, historical reality of globalization, seek to nuance their understanding of the historical process. It would be Luddite to resist irreversible advances in the globalization of science and technology, especially in the fields of communication and transport – advances that underpin the economic globalization – but it is equally short-sighted to fail to see how globalization is being adroitly packaged and presented. Sure, we can look forward to a world where Starbucks and Big Macs are always and everywhere available, but not to a world where everyone can afford good restaurants or tickets to top-league soccer games. Egalitarianism is as strictly controlled in the global village as it ever was, and the 'democratic capitalism' of the US no more includes poor blacks or migrant labourers from Mexico than the benefits of the globalized economy extend to the Third World as a whole. Globalization as a phenomenon of contemporary life, on the one hand, and the economic, neoliberal, fundamentalism of globalization on the other, are happily conjoined by those who seek to blur the distinction between a technological transformation and an ideology devoted to profit and to existing patterns of wealth distribution. The putative tenet of neoliberalism – an unregulated free market – is wilfully abandoned when politics dictate, as shown by the return to protectionism by the US in the steel industry in 2002. The free movement of goods around the world is heralded as a universal good, but the free movement of labour is rigorously curtailed and controlled in the interests of domestic political authority. And, all the time, the differentials in wealth between the haves and the have-nots are not only maintained, both within states and between countries, but solidified as never before.

Anarchism and the philosophy of Marx directly challenge what we are assiduously led to believe are inevitable and natural facts. The facts – that most of us are little more than our labour power, always in thrall to the laws of the market-place, that most things can be expressed in monetary terms, that the quality of life is related to the possession of commodities, that happiness best belongs to a private not public sphere – are not the result of some preordained human nature or natural metaphysic, but of history. The facts are historical, not only in the general sense of arising from contingent circumstances that could always be different, but arising from the particular history of capitalism in the West. We live in a world where the alienation described by Marx has had over a century to layer itself into human consciousness, or at least the consciousness of the global North. It requires the perspectives of Nietzsche, Foucault and others to shed some light on how capitalism creates a state of alienated being where the sense of self does not include the imagining of a different way of living. The possibility of changing the 'facts' is always there, though there is no assurance that change will make things better and anarchists do not ignore 'the potential – which lies in every culture and every human being – to centre life around that particularly Western mixture of greed and *naïveté*'.[1] To believe in libertarian socialism does not depend on a utopian belief in the perfectibility of human beings, just an appreciation of mutual aid and solidarity as basic principles for the betterment of life. In the same way, while anarchism means the abolition of government as a unitary coercive body, it is acutely aware of the need for government in terms of complex systems requiring organizing, administering and prioritizing. Anarchism cannot be simply uncorked and left to flow, and the abolition of imposed authority is not the same as absolute freedom, which in practice leads to exploitation and eventual domination by one group.

What anarchism rejects is the bourgeois mind-set that sees life as a game in some economic playground, with winners and losers. Anarchism shares with Marx the conviction that capitalism makes people unhappy and that the cause of alienation is the application of laws of supply and demand to human needs. Marx himself gave bleak expression to how this can reduce the quality of life to the point where a human 'feels that he is acting freely only in animal functions – eating, drinking and procreating, or at most in his dwelling and adornment – while in his human functions he is nothing more than an animal'.[2] He goes on to qualify this by acknowledging the genuine human value of eating, drinking and procreating and so on, but only to stress how, because they have become abstracted from other aspects of life, they become ends in themselves and lose their value. Anarchist literature, far more so than most Marxist tracts, engages viscerally with the ugly cheapening of life that modern capitalism and consumer culture has effected, and, just as Marx has his bleak moments, anarchists are sometimes attracted to apocalyptic modes that express their sense of horror. Dadaism, as Greil Marcus shows with a photograph of a German war victim alongside ones of Janco's masks and Hannah Höch's *Fröliche Dame*, can seem a sane and polite response to the obscenities of World War I.[3] When in 1966 Black Mask, an American anarchist group, called for the destruction of museums in a day of action against the Museum of Modern Art in New York, they subsequently published a statement explaining that they didn't mean the literal destruction of museums and their contents. The passion for destruction, as Bakunin famously said,[4] is also a creative urge, and these seemingly contrary feelings may coalesce and express themselves demonically, with the poetry buried under demotic tropes, as in the first wild rush of Punk in the mid-to-late '70s. What seemed to some like gleeful nihilism could be trenchant social and political criticism, aggressively confronting what is qualitatively absent from bourgeois ideals, and individuals like Jamie Reid, the 'art director' for The Sex Pistols, were very aware of the anarchist tradition in which they were working. The public responded by catapulting 'God Save the Queen' – a song to twin with Shelley's 'The Mask of Anarchy' for the verve of its anger – to the top of the charts despite massive censorship and a gerrymandering that officially placed The Sex Pistols' song in second place behind a Rod Stewart single.

The triumphant public success of 'God Save the Queen', in a royal jubilee year that was encouraging patriotic street parties, constituted just the kind of fissure opening in the system that Situationism had always anticipated. It seemed for a brief while that consumer culture would have difficulty in profiting from the feeling of 'Pretty vacant / And we don't care'. Though, sure enough, the fault line was repaired and market research learnt to milk apathy for all it was worth, the fracture pointed a way to a future that unwaveringly rejected the papering over of cracks that liberals offered. Sex Pistols' Punk rejected whole domains of bourgeois spectator life – shopping, tourism, music, politics – with a passion that was rooted in working-class experience. The theorizing came later, allowing the likes of the Socialist Workers' Party to try and cash in on Rock Against Racism (just as it now endeavours to cash in on the anti-capitalist movement), and the original anarchist spirit, in the words of Shane MacGowan, was diluted: 'You know, like The Clash, they turned it into a political thing. Started people thinking politically. Old hippies cut their hair, and got into it. It was the hippies' revenge on society. The true punks weren't interested in politics.'[5] Politics is predicated on a programme for the future, but Punk culture was about life as it is lived, not as it might be. This spirit of immediate revolt against the way things are is essential to anarchism's concern with how we live, how we behave and relate to others, how we dress and conduct ourselves. One of the graffiti that appeared on the walls of Paris in 1968 proclaimed 'Under the Paving Stones, the Beach!' and anarchists seek to tear up the reality that seems so concrete and enact an alternative in the here and now.

Anarchists, out of their passion for a better way of organizing life and their anger at the ease with which people so often bury their imagination and make ignoble compromises with the way things are, even convincing themselves that this is as good as it gets, often find themselves occupying negative positions. As Wilde said of Shelley, sometimes the note of rebellion is too strong and what is forgotten is that the perfect personality strives for peace not rebellion. Many of today's anarchists have learned this lesson, as shown by anti-capitalist protestors inverting forms of violent behaviour. The anti-capitalist movement, its mode of existence, is anarchism because anarchism is a process not an event. Revolution is not something that can or should be planned as an event because revolution is no longer defined of in terms of a violent, forceful overthrow of an existing order but seen instead as a deep change in our way of thinking about the exercise of power and the administration of government. The destructive aspect of traditional anarchism was bound up with the equally traditional idea of capturing political power in a revolutionary act. Such a destructive approach is, on the contrary, the hallmark of present-day global capitalism as it seeks to extend and strengthen its ideological control. Indeed, the challenge is to meet the realization that the US, to give the globalizing force of the free market a territorial label, will use massive violence to secure its control. And not just the US, for violence and state power always accompany one another, as shown by the willingness of state authorities to employ live ammunition against anti-capitalist protestors. In so far as the conduct of organized violence is inseparable from a hierarchical command structure, anarchism and pacifism may be inseparable. At the very same time, though, the issue of violence is something that state power is likely to define, and trying to ignore this by putting one's hands in the air, literally or metaphorically, may be self-deluding.

Anarchism offers a radical criticism of the way things are, and an equally radical vision of how things could be, but constantly needs to show it can offer a creditable programme for effecting a transition from one to the other. The new anarchism is anti-Party but, far from being unaware of the need to address the issue of political power, seeks to avoid the catastrophic mistakes of the past when the left placed its faith in the Party. Such faith, it now seems clear, ended up short-circuiting the very political and social conditions that were necessary for socialism; faith in leadership and the party machine became part of the problem and not the solution. There are political parties representing ideologies of the free market, liberal capitalism and state socialism that, if in a position of power, would set about introducing new legislation, as well as amending or dismantling existing legislation, in an attempt to implement their beliefs and policies. This is how they work. For many critics of anarchism, including ones sympathetic to libertarian socialism, there is perceived to be a constitutional weakness within anarchism that prevents it from being taken seriously as a political force because it does not work like this. For anarchists to say that the capture of seats in a parliament is not what it's about, and that voting is a sham, does not remove parliaments, politicians or the power they represent and exercise. For critics of anarchism this is tantamount to an admission of failure because such critics cannot conceive of power and politics in any other mode. The anarchist mode remains outside their field of vision. Just as it is a category mistake to think that anarchists don't believe in government – when what is at issue is the nature of government – it is equally mistaken to think that anarchists are opposed to party organization. What happened in Spain in the 1930s could not have taken place without an organized anarchist party, in the form of a mass trade union movement, and a machinery of administration. The anti-capitalist movement is not a party in the traditional sense but it represents the kind of decentralized, un-hierarchical organization that could forge links with labour movements and reinvent itself for future struggles. Similarly, while anarchists have always distrusted leaders, it would be doctrinaire to remain blind to the fact that some people come to the fore in many situations and charismatic indi-viduals do often emerge. The Zapatista movement, with its own highly charismatic Subcomandante Marcos, is well aware of the danger posed by any form of *caudillo* – a patriarch or local boss – and an early communiqué explained how ski-masks are worn not only for security but as a 'vaccine against *caudillismo*'.[6] Leaders are probably inevitable, and if a structure does not allow for, and accommodate, this, the alternative is going to be an informal, undemocratic leadership, a version of what the Class War Federation called the dictatorship of the big mouth.

Just as science is more than a list of facts and observations, so an-archism is more than a set of beliefs or principles. Traditional Marxism and socialism was a set of principles and, so the thinking went, it was a matter of obtaining state power and using it to implement those principles. This is a crude simplification, but it helps highlight anarchism's critical concern with the means as much as the end. The medium really is the message of anarchism. Freely creating non-hierarchical, decentralized organizations, federations and modes of behaviour *is* anarchism and this is what makes it revolutionary, not the storming of barricades (though it may be this as well). Emma Goldman spoke of anarchism as not a theory of the future but 'a living force in the affairs of our life, constantly creating new conditions . . . the spirit of revolt, in whatever form, against every-thing that hinders human growth'.[7] In this sense, anarchism is an *idea* not an opinion, a compass, a potential, an ambience, qualitative not quantita-tive, a desire to orientate the world and life's possibilities in terms of becoming and autonomy. The singularity of anarchism is its synthesis of a visionary, sensuous prospect of a better world with a cognitive Marxist philosophy, and a striving towards a radical psychology that offers a response to one of the central problems of politics: why does desire appar-ently submit so readily to its own repression? Anarchism is not waiting for a future, it does not rest on some millenarium gospel. Anarchism as a process, a means of existing, happens when people collaborate with others out of a felt need for justice, on a voluntary basis, and without degrees of rank or hierarchy. Such moments are often personal or small-group affairs but they can be public and they can point the way forward for libertarian socialism, providing a space and an orientation for human progress unshackled by a traditional state socialism that has reached a point like a chess position where a piece cannot be moved.

Anarchism is a tension. A tension between the way things are and the ways they could be, between being and becoming, despair and hope, between solitude and solidarity, between communism and individual-ism, Marx and Nietzsche, a tension between the power and the limitations of rationalism, between rejecting violence and acknowledg-ing the limits of pacifism. Anarchism is a tension in attitudes towards leadership, forms of organization and structures of government, a tension between creating present joys and preparing resistance to capi-talism, between the content of art and aesthetic forms. The new anarchism accepts and lives with the tension as a necessary and power-ful dynamic. John Barker, imprisoned at the age of 23 for the Angry Brigade campaign, recognizes an aspect of this tension as an aspect of his youth that need not be cast aside: 'To be serious about your beliefs and wanting a good time in the process may have been part of those innocent times but is not some eternal psychological impossibility, a contradiction written in stone.'[8] The Zapatista Marcos is able to play with the tension, using it to inject humour, realism and self-interrogation into the movement he is a part of. Some of his communiqués have taken the form of conversations with an hallucinatory jungle beetle named Durito able to question the movement, and Marcos has also whimsically adopted the role of a prosecutor levelling a series of charges against himself.[9] Indymedia seeks to challenge the hegemony of capitalism by using technology as a form of play and pleasure as well as work and activism. The anarchist tension is at the heart of anti-capitalist protests – visually, tactically and politically.

On a recent May Day at Enghave Plads. in Copenhagen, anarchists gathered to form their own contingent that fed into a much larger march across the city. It was a tame affair, too many bottles of Carlsberg around for any serious business, but the youthfulness of the participants was striking. An older man looking for his son, from a former relationship, whom he thought would turn up and was hoping to see again, remarked wistfully to me that anarchism was a dream, but that he loved his son all the more for having such a dream. Like Wilde's cartography, any map of the world without a place for An-archy is not worth using, but as a new pathway is being drawn through a world of global capitalism a new map is emerging in the process, and A marks the spot where Marx's appointment with anarchism needs to be made, the return to Marx through anarchism. Revolution is no longer to be seen only through the eyes of an Eisenstein; that historical moment has passed, and although it may come again there may also come a time when the events at Seattle 1999 and Genoa 2001 are seen to have inaugurated a new moment in history. This is not to predict the demise of capitalism for, although newspapers may commission obituaries before the personages expire, something does not die because its death notice is written in advance, and the anti-capitalist movement will have to reinvent itself in due course. State power was caught off guard in

Seattle but not in Genoa, and while levels of police surveillance and infiltration will increase to try and contain the anti-capitalist movement, its strength and power will not be so easy to disable – because of its anarchist nature.

They can shoot us now. Go ahead. They can put us in jail. Feel free. They can beat us. Do it, I've paid for better. They can throw us out of first-floor windows. But we can fly. They can say how it ain't on their monopoly media. Please do. They can equate our justice with their violence. Of course they will. They can draft in liberals to steal ideals. You know they'll try. They can ban us. Stop us. Fight us. Scare us. Kill us. They can close airports, stations, roads and minds. They can provoke and scheme. Cheat and prosper. Distort and destroy. They can create laws, more laws and by-laws to suit themselves. They can build bigger and better weapons to attack us with and to enrich their pals. They can sell us crap, sell us fear and sell us out. They can call us consumers not citizens. Apathetic not angry. Disinterested not disillusioned. They can make us despair and weep, fear and loathe, run and hide. They can take our work, our money and our lives. But we come with justice and fire. We come with honour and ideas. We come with decency and desire. We come now and we come as unstoppable as the rain. They can shoot us now. Go ahead.[10]

References

One: Global Anarchism

1 See, for example, the N30 Black Bloc statement (which can be found at various sites on the web, including www.infoshop.org/no2wto.html) explaining their action at Seattle. For a punchy account of what happened on the streets of Seattle in 1999, see Alexander Cockburn, Jefrey St Clair and Allan Sekula, *5 Days That Shook the World* (London, 2000), written soon after the event.
2 The most detailed account of the kind of thinking and grass roots activism that led up to Seattle is to be found in Benjamin Shepard and Ronald Hayduk, eds, *From Act Up to the WTO* (London, 2002). For the input by farmers, see the interview with José Bové, 'A Farmers' International', *New Left Review*, 12 (November–December 2001). For the anarchist nature of the anti-capitalist movement, see David Graeber, 'The New Anarchists', *New Left Review*, 13 (January–February 2002).
3 Graeber, 'The New Anarchists', p. 63.
4 Amorty Starr, *Naming the Enemy* (London, 2000), p. 223.
5 Joseph Conrad, *The Secret Agent* (London, 1997), p. 228.
6 Media reports in 1960 on the death of the non-fictional anarchist

Francisco Sabate, falsely alleged that his last words were *'Viva la muerte'* when he realized the police had no intention of taking him alive.

7 Errico Malatesta, *Anarchy* (London, 2001), p. 45.

8 'But just think how good communism is! The state won't bother us anymore'; attributed to Mao Zedong in 1919, quoted in Ross Terrill, *Mao: A Biography* (London, 1980), chap. 4.

9 See, Tim Jordan, *Activism!* (London, 2002), chap. 6. For Indymedia's DIY media centres see, for example, www.uk.indymedia.org and Ana Nogueira, 'The Birth and Promise of the Indymedia Revolution', in Shepard and Hayduk, *From Act Up to the WTO*, pp. 290–97.

10 David Ronfeldt, John Arquilla, Graham E. Fuller, Melissa Fuller, *The Zapatista Social Netwar in Mexico* (Santa Monica, 1998).

11 Ronfeldt et al., *The Zapatista Social Netwar*, p. 70.

12 Peter Marshall, *Demanding the Impossible* (London, 1993), chaps 4–10. For the most comprehensive source of anarchist writings, see www.akuk.com

Two: Anarchos

1 The difficulty of just such a project is examined in Jens Bartelson, *The Critique of the State* (Cambridge 2001).

2 Proudhon, *General Idea of the Revolution in the Nineteenth Century*, trans. J. B. Robinson (London, 1923), p. 294.

3 Available from Indymedia, PO Box 587, London SW2 4HA, UK. Imc-uk-video@lists.indymedia.org

4 Allen J. Beck and Paige M. Harrison, 'Prisoners in 2000', *Bureau of Justice Statistics Bulletin (2001)*, www.ojp.usdoj.gov/bjs/pub/pdf/p00.pdf

5 For the United States's 'disappeared', see *The Independent* (26 February 2002).

6 Of the adult population eligible to vote in Britain in 2001, 8 per cent

were not registered and of the 92 per cent who were registered, 57 per cent turned out. Of the 57 per cent, some 42 per cent voted New Labour, making Blair's 'majority' 21.8 per cent of the vote. The US election in 2000 yielded a similar result.

7 M. Bakunin, *God and the State* (London, 1883), quoted in George Woodcock, *The Anarchist Reader* (Sussex, 1977), p. 313.

8 The story of the experiments that produced such alarming evidence of the degree to which people will accept authority is told in Stanley Milgram, *Obedience to Authority* (London, 1974).

9 Alex Comfort, *Against Power and Death* (London, 1994) p. 13.

10 Oscar Wilde, *The Soul of Man Under Socialism* (London, 1891), reprinted in Linda Dowling, ed., *The Soul of Man Under Socialism and Selected Critical Prose* (London, 2001), p. 130. For a dramatization of Wilde's anarchism, see Terry Eagleton, *Saint Oscar and Other Plays* (Oxford, 1997).

11 Peter Kropotkin, *Anarchism and Anarchist Communism*, ed. Nicholas Walter (London, 1987), p. 8. This includes a reprint of the article for *Encyclopaedia Britannica* that first appeared in 1910 and continued in successive editions until 1960.

12 Wilde, *The Soul of Man Under Socialism*, p. 13.

13 In Britain, an estimated 1.5 million CCTV cameras record the comings and goings of citizens, with Londoners being caught on camera about 300 times a day, and face-recognition software already in place in the London Borough of Newham: *The Sunday Times* (16 June 2002). CCTV cameras have also been installed in the cells of some prison blocks/segregation units.

14 Paul Rainbow, ed., *The Foucault Reader* (London, 1984), p. 22.

15 Max Stirner, *The Ego and Its Own*, ed. David Leopold (Cambridge, 1995), p. 148. The book was first published in Germany in late 1844 (with 1845 on the title-page) as *Der Einzige und Sein Eigentum*.

16 Murray Bookchin, *Social Anarchism or Lifestyle Anarchism* (Edinburgh

and San Francisco, 1995).

17 George Bradford, 'Civilization in Bulk', *Fifth Estate* (Spring, 1991), quoted in Murray Bookchin, *Social Anarchism or Lifestyle Anarchism*, pp. 36–7.

18 See World Rainforest Movement and Sahabat Alam Malaysia, *The Battle for Sarawak's Forests* (Penang, 1990) and Bruno Manser, *Voices from the Rainforest* (Selangor, 1996).

19 John Moore, 'A Primitivist Primer' at www.primitivism.com offers a succinct account. See also John Zerzan, *Future Primitive* (New York, 1994).

20 Martin Heidegger, *The Question Concerning Technology and Other Essays* (New York, 1977).

21 The Unabomber's Manifesto is available on the web at various sites, including www.time.com/time/reports/unabomber

22 Peter Kropotkin, *The Conquest of Bread* (London, 1990), p. 27, pp. 29–30.

23 See, for example, Harold Barclay, *People Without Government* (London, 1982).

24 See Frank Fernandez, *Cuban Anarchism: The History of a Movement* (Tucson, AZ, 2001).

25 For a recent expression of this attitude, see John Lloyd, *The Protest Ethic: How the Anti-Globalisation Movement Challenges Social Democracy* (London, 2001).

26 Errico Malatesta, *Anarchy* (London, 2001), p. 40.

27 Malatesta, *Anarchy*, p. 40.

28 Le Guin, *The Dispossessed*, p. 138.

29 Le Guin, *The Dispossessed*, p. 54.

30 Le Guin, *The Dispossessed*, p. 256.

31 Eric Hobsbawm, *Bandits* (London, 2000), pp. 124–5.

Three: Marx, Nietzsche and Anarchism

1 See, for example, a Spartacist pamphlet of the International Communist League, 'Marxism vs. Anarchism' (New York, 2001), which concludes how 'it would be a travesty if [anarchism] . . . were permitted to deflect a new generation of would-be revolutionaries from the crucial task which remains before us: the building of a revolutionary leadership rooted in the proletariat, a Leninist vanguard party' (p. 55).

2 For a 'jolly good fun' approach to the Bakunin–Marx split, see Francis Wheen, *Karl Marx* (London, 1999), chap. 11. For a more seasoned view, David McLellan, *Karl Marx* (London, 1981), chap. 7, and for an anarchist analysis Marcus Graham, *Marxism and a Free Society* (Orkney, 1981). For Bakunin's extraordinary character and his clash with Marx: Edmund Wilson, *To the Finland Station* (London, 1974), chap. 14.

3 Georg Lukács, 'The Antinomies of Bourgeois Thought', *History and Class Consciousness* (London, 1968), p. 127. This was a path Kant did not follow, despite the problem of trying to reconcile his rationalism – regarding the world as out there, independent of us and governed by natural laws – with other ideas that Kant needed, such as the freedom of the ethical will. How can we ethically act on and affect a world that we can only ever be rational observers of? And given the supremacy of rationality, what can be made of the Kantian 'thing in itself', the ultimate nature of things which remains necessarily beyond our grasp? This too must be part of the natural world, but it must remain outside the *a priori* structure of rationality.

4 Karl Marx, *The German Ideology*, ed. C. J. Arthur (London, 1974), p. 47.

5 Karl Marx, *Early Writings*, trans. R. Livingstone and G. Benton (Harmondsworth, 1975), p. 390.

6 Karl Marx, 'Theses on Fuerbach', in Marx and Engels, *Basic Writings on Politics and Philosophy*, ed. Lewis S. Feuer (London, 1969), p. 286.

7 Karl Marx, *The Communist Manifesto* (London, 1998), p. 37.

8 Marx, *Early Writings*, p. 257.

9 Marx, *Early Writings*, p. 328.

10 Thomas Hobbes, *Leviathan*, ed. R Tuck (Cambridge, 1991), I. XIII. 9.

11 Marx, *Early Writings*, p. 324.

12 *The Independent* (9 January 2002), p. 1. For literary fast food, see Andrew Blake, *The Irresistible Rise of Harry Potter: Kid-Lit in a Globalised World* (London, 2002).

13 Marx, *Early Writings*, p. 361.

14 See Karl Korsch, *Marxism and Philosophy* (London, 1970), pp. 113–22. For a similar development in Soviet film aesthetics, Peter Wollen, *Signs and Meaning in the Cinema* (London, 1998), pp. 10–47.

15 Friedrich Nietzsche, 'Of Self-Overcoming', *Thus Spake Zarathrusta* (London, 1969), p. 138

16 Friedrich Nietzsche, *The Gay Science* (Cambridge, 2001), aphorism 354.

17 Friedrich Nietzsche, *On the Genealogy of Morality* (Cambridge, 1996), p. 62.

18 'The meaningless of suffering, not the suffering itself, was the curse which has so far blanketed mankind – and the ascetic ideal offered man a meaning!' Nietzsche, *Genealogy of Morality*, p. 127.

19 'We loathe the Church, not its poison . . . Apart from the Church, we too love the poison;' Nietzsche, *Genealogy of Morality*, p. 21.

20 'The concept of "thing" is merely a reflex of the faith in the ego as cause . . . And even your atom, my dear *messieurs*, mechanists and physicists – how much error, how much rudimentary psychology still remains in your atom. To say nothing of the "thing in itself", that *horrendum pudendum* of the metaphysicians!' Friedrich Nietzsche, 'The Four Great Errors', *Twilight of the Idols/The Anti-Christ* (London 1990), p. 61.

21 'No things remain but only dynamic quanta in a relation of tension to other dynamic quanta: their essence lies in their relation to all other

quanta;' Friedrich Nietzsche, *The Will to Power* (London, 1984),
   aphorism 635.

22 Friedrich Nietzsche, *Daybreak* (Cambridge, 1982), aphorism 175.

23 Nietzsche, *The Gay Science*, aphorism 329.

24 See Max O. Hallman, 'Nietzsche's Environmental Ethics',
   Environmental Ethics, 13 (Summer 1991); and, Ralph R. Acampora,
   'Using and Abusing Nietzsche for Environmental Ethics',
   Environmental Ethics, 16 (Summer 1994).

25 Quoted in Alison Blunt and Jane Wills, *Dissident Geographies* (Harlow,
   2000), p. 15.

Four: Attacking the State

1 Eric Hobsbawm, *Bandits* (London, 2000), p. 121.

2 Peter Marshall, *Demanding the Impossible* (London, 1993), p. 97. See also
   W. H. Armytage, *Heavens Below: Utopian Experiments in England
   1560–1690* (London, 1961).

3 Gerrard Winstanley, *The Law of Freedom and other Writings*,
   ed. Christopher Hill (Cambridge, 1983), p. 128.

4 Winstanley, *Freedom and other Writings*, p. 78.

5 Winstanley, *Freedom and other Writings*, p. 159.

6 Marshall, *Demanding the Impossible*, pp. 102–7. For more on the
   Ranters, see A. L. Morton, *The World of the Ranters* (London 1970);
   for the seventeenth-century left-wing Republican groups more generally, see Christopher Hill, *The World Turned Upside Down: Radical
   Ideas During the English Revolution* (London, 1972).

7 Quoted in Marshall, *Demanding the Impossible*, p. 105.

8 Alison Brunt and Jane Wills, *Dissident Geographies* (Harlow, 2000),
   pp. 26–7.

9 Quoted in Marshall, *Demanding the Impossible*, p. 432.

10 James Joll, *The Anarchists* (London, 1979), p. 27.

11 Joll, *The Anarchists*, p. 28.

12 Alexander Berkman, *Prison Memoirs of an Anarchist* (Pittsburgh, 1970), p. 432.

13 See Voline [pseud. for V. M. Eichenbaum], *The Unknown Revolution* (Detroit 1974), Bk III, Pt. 1, chap. 4.

14 Gregory Petrovich Maximoff, *The Guillotine at Work*, vol. I: *The Leninist Counter-Revolution* (Orkney, 1979), p. 168.

15 Voline, *The Unknown Revolution*, p. 628.

16 Voline, *The Unknown Revolution*, p. 315. See also Peter Arshinov, *History of the Makhnovist Movement* (Detroit, 1975).

17 See, Frank Fernandez, *Cuban Anarchism: The History of a Movement* (Tucson, AZ, 2001).

18 David Miller, *Anarchism* (London, 1984), p. 105.

19 Joll, *The Anarchists*, p. 239.

20 Miller, *Anarchism*, pp. 162–3, and Gaston Leval, 'Self Management in Action', *A New World in our Hearts*, ed. Albert Meltzer (Orkney, 1978).

21 George Orwell, *Homage to Catalonia* (London, 1989), pp. 3–4. Orwell's account echoes a firsthand description of the Paris Commune of 1871 recorded by Kropotkin: 'I will never forget those delightful moments of deliverance. I came down from my upper chamber in the Latin Quarter to join the immense open-air club which filled the boulevards of Paris from one end to the other. Everyone talked about public affairs; all mere personal preoccupations were forgotten; no more was thought of buying or selling; all felt ready, body and soul, to advance towards the future. Men of the middle-class even, carried away by the general enthusiasm, saw with joy a new world opened up. "If it is necessary to make a social revolution," they said, "make it then. Put all things in common; we are ready for it."' Quoted in Jeff Ferrell, *Tearing Down the Streets Adventures in Urban Anarchy* (New York, 2000), p. 242.

22 Brian Bamford, 'Interview with Ken Loach', *The Raven*, 9, no. 1 (London, 1996); see also Bamford's interview with Jim Allen in the same issue.

23 Speaking of Francisco Sabate: 'Just as there are women who are only fully themselves in bed, so there are some men who only realise themselves in action'. Eric Hobsbawm, *Bandits* (London, 2000), pp. 125–38. For a more sympathetic account, Antonio Tellez, *Sabate*, trans. Stuart Christie (London, 1974).

24 Daniel and Gabriel Cohn-Bendit, *Obsolete Communism* (Edinburgh, 2000), p. 54 (first published in 1968).

25 Cohn-Bendit, *Obsolete Communism*, pp. 55–6.

26 Hilary Creek, released in 1977 a few months after Anna Mendelson, now lives abroad. Mendelson is now an acclaimed poet, under a new name. John Barker and Jim Greenfield became involved in a cannabis smuggling operation after their release, were arrested and imprisoned again. There is a brief, firsthand, but cautiously unrevealing account of the trial in Stuart Christie, *The Christie File* (Orkney, 1980). The best account of the Angry Brigade campaign is found in John Barker's review of a book on the subject, available on line at www.christiebooks.com

27 All quotations from Angry Brigade statements are from *Conspiracy Notes 4*, Stoke Newington Eight Defence Group (London, 1972).

28 Errico Malatesta, *Anarchy* (London, 2001), pp. 10–11.

29 [No author named], *Armed Resistance in West Germany* (London, 1972), p. 60.

30 [No author named], *Red Army Faction* (San Francisco, 1979), p. 1.

31 *Red Army Faction*, p. 1.

32 *Red Army Faction*, p. 3. The statement was issued after Baader was liberated from armed guards at a library where he had permission to study after his capture a month earlier in West Berlin.

33 Quoted in *The Leveller*, no. 10 (London, 1977), pp. 11–12.

34 Ulrike Meinhof, 'Armed Anti-Imperialistic Struggle', in Chris Claus and Sylvère Lotringer, eds, *Hatred of Capitalism* (Los Angeles, 2001), p. 63.

35 George Woodcock, *Gandhi* (London, 1972), pp. 85–6.

36 Woodcock, *Gandhi*, pp. 85–6.

37 [No author named], *On Fire: The Battle of Genoa and the Anti-capitalist Movement* (Edinburgh 2002), p. 5.

38 *On Fire*, p. 48.

39 *Class War* (undated).

40 *Class War* (undated).

41 Class War Collective, *Unfinished Business*, (Stirling, 1992).

42 *Class War*, issue 73 (Summer 1997), p. 9 (available through www.akuk.com). Since the 1997 split, a new Class War Federation and *Class War* newspaper have appeared.

43 Zapatista takes its name from the Mexican anarchist rebel Emiliano Zapata; see Marshall, *Demanding the Impossible*, pp. 511–13.

44 Días Tello, *La Rebellión de las Cañadas* (Mexico City, 1995), quoted in David Ronfeldt, John Arquilla, Graham E. Fuller and Melissa Fuller, *The Zapatista Social Netwar in Mexico* (Santa Monica, 1998), p. 33.

45 Quoted in Amory Starr, *Naming the Enemy* (London, 2000), p. 104.

Five: Subverting Hierarchies

1 Max Stirner, *The Ego and Its Own* (Cambridge, 1995), p. 148.

2 Karl Marx, *The Communist Manifesto* (London, 1998), p. 37.

3 Quoted in Len Bracken, *Guy Debord, Revolutionary* (Los Angeles, 1997), p. 27.

4 These terms from Situationist texts are taken from Stewart Home, *The Assault on Culture* (Edinburgh, 1991), pp. 18, 29, 30.

5 Debord dismissed individualist anarchism as 'laughable' and

anarchism generally as being marred by its focus on the conclusion of revolutionary struggle rather than the method, it is the 'ideology of pure liberty' which equalises everything. (The quotes are from Guy Debord, *Society of the Spectacle* (Detroit, 1970, revised edition 1983), sections 92–4 of chap. 4. The book is available on the web at www.nothingness.org) Bakunin was accused of elevating his opinions into an authoritarianism just like Marx. At the same time, though, Debord acknowledged the social revolution in Spain in 1936 as the most advanced achievement of working people in history.

6 See Bracken, *Guy Debord*, pp. 114–19.

7 For more on the Dutch Provos, Kommune 1, as well as other activists' movements of the 1960s, for example the Motherfuckers, Yippies and White Panthers, see Home, *The Assault on Culture*, chap. 12.

8 See also Jon Savage, *England's Dreaming: Anarchy, Sex Pistols, Punk Rock and Beyond* (New York, 1991) and Neil Nehring, *Flowers in the Dustbin: Culture, Anarchy, and Postwar England* (Ann Arbor, MI, 1993).

9 Jeff Ferrell, *Tearing Down the Streets Adventures in Urban Anarchy* (New York, 2001), chap. 6.

10 William Blake, 'The Marriage of Heaven and Hell', *Collected Poems* (Oxford, 1968), pp. 149–50.

11 William Blake, line 152 of Night the Ninth in 'The Four Zoas', *Collected Poems*, p. 361.

12 Wilhelm Reich, *The Mass Psychology of Fascism* (London, 1977), p. 332.

13 Reich, *Mass Psychology of Fascism*, p. 337.

14 Reich, *Mass Psychology of Fascism*, p. 342.

15 Richard Porton, *Film and the Anarchist Imagination* (London, 1999), pp. 162–4.

16 Francisco Aranda, *Luis Buñuel: A Critical Biography*, trans. and ed. David Robinson (New York, 1976), p. 76, quoted in Porton, *Film and the Anarchist Imagination*, p. 238.

17 Roger Cardinal and Robert Stuart Short, *Surrealism* (London, 1973), p. 123.

18 Quoted in Cardinal and Short, *Surrealism*, p. 36; taken from the Second Surrealist Manifesto.

19 Allan Antliff, *Anarchist Modernism* (Chicago, 2001).

20 Quoted in Antliff, *Anarchist Modernism*, p. 213.

21 This becomes very apparent in David Weir, *Anarchy and Culture: The Aesthetic Politics of Modernism* (Amhurst, MA, 1997) which depends entirely for its argument (that while anarchism failed politically it succeeded culturally in American modernist aesthetics) on a very limited notion of anarchism in terms of extreme individualism. See also chap. 32 of Peter Marshall, *Demanding the Impossible* (London, 1993), for a succinct summary of anarchism in the USA.

22 Antliff, *Anarchist Modernism*, p. 176.

23 See Porton, *Film and the Anarchist Imagination*, pp. 244–5. See also www.subgenius.com and Home *The Assault on Culture*, pp. 93–4. For accounts of other such jests, some more entertaining than the Church of the SubGenius, see V. Vale and Andrea Juno, eds, *Pranks* (San Francisco, 1988), and Ron Sakolsky and Fred Wei-Han Ho, eds, *Sounding Off with CD* (New York, 1995).

24 Vale and Juno, *Pranks*, p. 4.

25 Bill Talen, Aka Reverend Billy, 'Wednesday, July 12: invasions of three NYC Starbucks', Benjamin Shepard and Ronald Hayduk, *From Act Up to the WTO* (London, 2002), pp. 316–19.

26 Murray Bookchin, *Social Anarchism or Lifestyle Anarchism* (Edinburgh and San Francisco, 1995), p. 3. For more of Bookchin's attacks on postmodernism, see his *Anarchism, Marxism, and the Future of the Left* (Edinburgh and San Francisco, 1999), pp. 115–42.

27 Lewis Call, 'Anarchy in the Matrix: Postmodern Anarchism in the Novels of William Gibson and Bruce Sterling', *Anarchist Studies*, 7, no. 2 (Cambridge, 1999), p. 100.

28 Samuel R. Delaney, *The American Shore: Meditations on a Tale of Science Fiction by Thomas M. Disch – 'Angouleme'* (New York, 1978), quoted in *Anarchist Review*, 7, no. 2, pp. 96–7.

29 Bruce Sterling, *Holy Fire* (London, 1997), p. 166.

30 William Gibson, *Idoru* (London, 1997), p. 221.

31 Call, 'Anarchy in the Matrix', p. 116.

32 *The London Review of Books*, 24, no. 7 (London, 2002), p. 22.

Six: The Anarchist Tension

1 Peter Høeg *Miss Smilla's Feeling for Snow* (London, 1996), p. 316.

2 Karl Marx, *Early Writings* (Harmondsworth, 1975), p. 327.

3 Greil Marcus, *Lipstick Traces* (London, 1990), p. 223.

4 Michael Bakunin, *Selected Writings* (New York, 1974), p. 58.

5 Victoria Mary Clarke and Shane MacGowan, *A Drink with Shane MacGowan* (London, 2001), p. 157.

6 Zapatista communiqué,6 January 1994, quoted in Bill Weinberg, *Homage to Chiapas* (London, 2002), p. 198.

7 Emma Goldman, *Anarchism and Other Essays*, intro. Richard Drinnon (New York, 1969), p. 63.

8 www.christiebooks.com

9 'The *machistas* accuse him of being feminist: guilty

The feminists accuse him of being *machista*: guilty

The Communists accuse him of being anarchist: guilty . . .

The "historic vanguard" accuses him of appealing to civil society and not the proletariat: guilty . . .

The adults accuse him of being a child: guilty

The children accuse him of being an adult: guilty . . .

The orthodox leftists accuse him of not condemning homosexuals and lesbians: guilty'

from *La Jornada* [Mexico City] (5 May 1995),
quoted in Bill Weinberg, *Homage to Chiapas*, p. 201.
10 Adam Porter, 'Year Zero', www.yearzero.org